AI FOR DIGITAL WARFARE

AI FOR EVERYTHING

Artificial intelligence (AI) is all around us. From driverless cars to game winning computers to fraud protection, AI is already involved in many aspects of life, and its impact will only continue to grow in future. Many of the world's most valuable companies are investing heavily in AI research and development, and not a day goes by without news of cutting-edge breakthroughs in AI and robotics.

The AI for Everything series will explore the role of AI in contemporary life, from cars and aircraft to medicine, education, fashion and beyond. Concise and accessible, each book is written by an expert in the field and will bring the study and reality of AI to a broad readership including interested professionals, students, researchers, and lay readers.

AI for Immunology
Louis J. Catania

AI for Cars
Hanky Sjafrie & Josep Aulinas

AI for Digital Warfare
Niklas Hageback & Daniel Hedblom

AI for Arts
Niklas Hageback & Daniel Hedblom

AI for Creativity
Niklas Hageback

AI for Fashion
Anthony Brew, Ralf Herbrich,
Christopher Gandrud, Roland Vollgraf,
Reza Shirvany & Ana Peleteiro Ramallo

AI for Death and Dying
Maggi Savin-Baden

AI for Radiology
Oge Marques

AI for Games
Ian Millington

AI for School Teachers
Rose Luckin & Karine George

AI for Learners
Carmel Kent, Benedict du Boulay &
Rose Luckin

AI for Social Justice
Alan Dix and Clara Crivellaro

For more information about this series please visit:
https://www.routledge.com/AI-for-Everything/book-series/AIFE

AI FOR DIGITAL WARFARE

NIKLAS HAGEBACK

DANIEL HEDBLOM

CRC Press

Taylor & Francis Group

Boca Raton   London   New York

CRC Press is an imprint of the
Taylor & Francis Group, an **informa** business

First Edition published 2022
by CRC Press
6000 Broken Sound Parkway NW, Suite 300, Boca Raton, FL 33487-2742

and by CRC Press
2 Park Square, Milton Park, Abingdon, Oxon, OX14 4RN

CRC Press is an imprint of Taylor & Francis Group, LLC

Library of Congress Cataloging-in-Publication Data
Names: Hageback, Niklas, author. | Hedblom, Daniel, author.
Title: AI for digital warfare / Niklas Hageback, Daniel Hedblom.
Description: First edition. | Boca Raton : CRC Press, 2021. | Includes
bibliographical references and index.
Identifiers: LCCN 2021008444 | ISBN 9781032048710 (hardback) |
ISBN 9781032048703 (paperback) | ISBN 9781003194965 (ebook)
Subjects: LCSH: Cyberspace operations (Military science) | Artificial
intelligence—War use.
Classification: LCC U167.5.C92 H34 2021 | DDC 355.4—dc23
LC record available at https://lccn.loc.gov/2021008444

ISBN: 978-1-032-04871-0 (hbk)
ISBN: 978-1-032-04870-3 (pbk)
ISBN: 978-1-003-19496-5 (ebk)

Typeset in Joanna
by codeMantra

To the Finnish Second lieutenant Simo Häyhä (1905 – 2002), a.k.a. The White Death (Valkoinen kuolema), the most formidable sniper the world has ever seen with an estimated 500 kills in less than 100 days of fighting during the Winter War of 1939 – 1940 against communist Soviet Union. He serves as one of the best examples of the combination of ingenuity and providence that seems to bestow righteous people that decide to stand up against evil. Indeed, a role model that embodies the virtues also required by the digital warriors fighting totalitarianism.

CONTENTS

CONTENTS

AUTHORS

Niklas Hageback has an extensive background in digital transformations and risk management. He has held regional executive management and project oversight roles at leading banks, including Credit Suisse, Deutsche Bank, and Goldman Sachs, in both Asia and Europe, where he was in charge of a number of complex regionwide digital transformation and risk management initiatives. More recently, he has done extensive work in Artificial Intelligence, notably machine learning, leading the development of automated human reasoning and computational creativity applications. He is a published author with bestsellers including *The Mystery of Market Movements: An Archetypal Approach to Investment Forecasting and Modelling* (2014), *The Virtual Mind: Designing the Logic to Approximate Human Thinking* (2017), *The Death Drive: Why Societies Self-Destruct* (2020), and *Leadership in the Digital Age: Renaissance of the Renaissance Men* (2020). He has also published a number of research papers in AI and finance.

Daniel Hedblom's background includes working as a senior artificial intelligence consultant developing data warehouses, data analytics, and visualisation tools. His focus has been on designing predictive analytic systems and models for financial markets and replicating consumer purchasing patterns with a core competence in the understanding and execution of the full project life cycle, and in particular database and data flow designs.

INTRODUCTION

Das Wissen muss ein Können werden.

Knowledge must become a skill.

Carl von Clausewitz (1780–1831)

legendary German war strategist

With the currently unprecedented pace of technological innovations, we humans, now as always, something which history well testifies to, will eventually also weaponise these new contraptions. From where does this compulsion to constantly seek to improve our capacity for destruction come from? Is there some perverted inclination to develop arms of everything we can get our hands on, or is it possibly just our deep-rooted survival instinct at play, triggering an urge to make sure we are at all times better armed than seemingly threatening tribes? Regardless of reason, we can notice how this generation of technical milestones are also being weaponised, and whether we like it or not, it heralds yet another new era of warfare. This also includes innovations in artificial intelligence (AI), which are one of the most talked about but probably least understood of the emerging new technologies.

To our traditional split of armed forces – army, navy, and, from the early twentieth century onwards, air force – over the last couple of decades, the capability to also engage in digital warfare can be added. Thus, questions need to be asked: Do we as humans really know what we are doing when we are developing a digital arsenal? Is it holding the propensity to change warfare in a way we have not been able to fully fathom yet? Are there unpleasant surprises of a collateral-damage nature lurking? How *exactly* do AI applications and tools introduce unique capacities that can be deployed in a military capacity? These are queries being pondered upon by war scientists in academia and war strategists in the armed forces throughout the world. It is, to say the least, a frontier science where most queries are open ended but are of such vital importance that they beget answers. When its potential capabilities have been fully ascertained and understood, it might come with profound insights that will change our perspective on warfare for the foreseeable future.

But before seeking to answer these questions, it is maybe useful to take a few steps back. The proverbial father of modern warfare, Carl von Clausewitz, immortalised through his still widely read work *On War*, which dates back two centuries, is best known for his broad-brushed strategic advice, narrated through a political perspective. His strategies have been generic enough to have stood the test of time (which is perhaps the reason), and quite naturally have included a wide range of interpretations. Hence, modern strategic approaches have and are still taking cues from his writings. One of these is *Blitzkrieg*. Blitzkrieg is an interesting concept. The origin of the word is somewhat controversial, but its deployment was pretty straightforward, albeit for the time unconventional. It was a mixing and matching of armed capabilities seeking to optimise their force, often against a superior opponent, by finding the opportunity to break through a weak point in the defence line, *schwerpunkt*, thereby achieving victory quickly and decisively. Speed and the element of surprise were key factors in seeking to create a sensation of shock, which would break the enemy's will to fight. Thus, psychology played a decisive part in whether such audacious ventures would be successful. It is interesting to note that in our times it is not exclusively the capacity of a military arsenal that decides the outcome of armed conflicts. A case in point are the nuclear deterrents that have simply become politically impossible to actually use. This also goes for more conventional approaches, such as carpet bombings, a preferred tactic during the Second World War and the Vietnam War. Instead, over time, the reliance on non-military means seeking to gain an advantage over an adversary, and ultimately forcing him to surrender, have advanced considerably. Many of these tactics are collectively labelled as psychological warfare. In essence, psychological warfare seeks to, through the utilisation of a variety of means typically in combination, break down the enemy's will to act and defend himself. Usually, the creation of confusion and shock are the effects sought after to make resistance appear to be a futile endeavour. With AI tools becoming increasingly advanced, and in many cases more human-like, their potential in psychological warfare are being recognised, which means digital warfare can move beyond just shutting down IT systems into more all-encompassing hybrid war strategies.

There is, however, a profound difference between the wars of yesteryear, which were mainly interstate affairs. Today, these are notably rarer, and instead there are proxy wars, grey zone conflicts, and undefinable blurred criminal activities cum warfare where commercial entities in a larger degree are being affected. This has made the dichotomies war–peace and friend–foe much harder to establish. What are you to do if an enemy you do not even know you have covertly starts to engage in hostile activities? A war against you can be lost before you even knew it started. These are scenarios that fall far outside known rules of engagements, but which have become increasingly frequent. And as any senior executive in any industry in any country will tell you, attacks and threats in the digital sphere top the list of risks they worry most about, no doubt having rendered them many sleepless nights. Digital capabilities to cause damage and destruction have taken us to unchartered territories. How can we defend ourselves against an invisible and unnamed enemy with the advantage of having both the timing and maybe the tools on their side? It has become a business-critical concern that can irreparably destroy an otherwise flourishing firm in an incredibly short time. This brings us to the gist of this book, namely how the weaponising of AI can and will change how warfare is being conducted, and what impact it will have on the corporate world. *AI for Digital Warfare* is structured in five chapters.

CHAPTER 1: PRINCIPLES OF WAR: CLAUSEWITZ AND BEYOND

Taking a starting point from Clausewitz's work on warfare, and how it has been practically applied, this chapter provides a backdrop on how the thinking about how to conduct war has been evolving, but also how it has remained steadfast to certain principles over the centuries. The blitzkrieg approach (coordinated efforts between air force, tanks, and infantry, and the psychological effect these surprise attacks had) was a deliberate part of the strategy. After the Second World War, there have been targeted efforts to do more with less, introducing special forces that, in small numbers, have been able to create havoc previously only expected from significantly larger numbers of troops. It is in this context, alternative means of conducting war, beyond bombs and bullets, are now playing a more important role than ever, and digital warfare is part of this. This chapter provides a context on why we are where we are on the principles of warfare, this to gauge a better understanding on what to expect next.

CHAPTER 2: WELCOME TO THE MURKY WORLD OF PSYCHOLOGICAL WARFARE

Psychological operations have always been part of warfare. However, it was really first from the Second World War that the tools of psychological warfare became more distinctly formalised and systematically organised. So, what it is really? What does it seek to achieve? And what tools does it utilise? This chapter will discuss the history of psychological warfare and where it is today, as well as to describe how it is deployed, both standalone and integrated into a broader strategy where information plays a key role.

CHAPTER 3: WHAT IS DIGITAL WARFARE?

As the world, through digital transformations, is moving much of its activities into the digital sphere, war, the most intrinsic part of human nature, has of course been bound to follow. This chapter will highlight and discuss known strategies and tools that have so far been utilised in digital warfare.

CHAPTER 4: WEAPONISING AI

This is a chapter that is impossible to lock down in time as the development and usage of new AI techniques are being introduced in an accelerating pace, and, at the time of print, some aspects might already be obsolete. However, there are fundamental design and development tenets that the coming generation of AI will deploy, which provide insights on what the weaponised versions can be capable of. How these can be integrated into digital warfare strategies is thoroughly described.

CHAPTER 5: BLITZKRIEG IN THE DIGITAL AGE

The wars of today are often nothing like the wars of the past. In fact, they are often not even called wars, yet the objective appears timeless, namely forcing one's will upon an adversary. War theorists talk about asymmetric or non-linear warfare, but is that what is happening now? Does the weaponisation of AI fit in this context or is it something altogether different? This chapter provides a playbook of realised and, as of yet, hypothetical strategies on how offensive digital warfare will be conducted, and surprisingly enough there are significant elements of both Clausewitz and blitzkrieg in them. An understanding of what is going on and what to expect will empower corporate leadership with insights of an unpleasant reality they might not wish existed, but, by being forewarned, they are forearmed to counter an unprecedented and formidable digital threat capable of annihilating a hapless adversary.

1

PRINCIPLES OF WAR: CLAUSEWITZ AND BEYOND

Aus ihnen wird sich ein gewisser *Schwerpunkt*, ein Zentrum der Kraft und Bewegung bilden, von welchem das Ganze abhängt, und auf diesen *Schwerpunkt* des Gegners muß der gesammelte Stoß aller Kräfte gerichtet sein

Out of these characteristics a certain center of gravity develops, the hub of all power and movement, on which everything depends. That is the point against which all our energies should be directed

Carl von Clausewitz (1780–1831),
legendary German war strategist

War is a messy business, no matter how meticulous one tries to plan for a military campaign, things are bound to go wrong. History is full of cases of the many unforeseen events that suddenly have turned the fortunes on the battlefield. In fact, even defining war is not all that straightforward, strange as it has been such an integral part of human history that has shaped many of the conditions we now are having to adhere to. Maybe this propensity to so readily be prepared to engage in violence is simply part of our DNA, highlighted as a manifest of our survival instinct to make sure we stay ahead of rivalling tribes in the quest for food, women, and whatever that ensures our biological survival. War is by some perceived as an efficient, albeit crude, tool to solve problems, but unfortunately being applied far too often and not unusually on issues not really suitable for military solutions, at least not in the long term. Beyond the deaths and destructions that war brings with it, it also has other, perhaps equally detrimental, consequences. To unleash a wave of violence, even if attempting to rigidly control it, comes with moral, cultural, and social repercussions that inevitably will spill over to areas outside the battlefield. It is said that starting a war is easy but ending it is not, there is certainly no lack of evidence of the fallouts from war spanning over generations. Whilst war for the sheer sake of it does occur, organised sadistic joyrides of that sort are thankfully exceptions, instead they generally serve as an instrument to achieve economic and/or political objectives. Thus, a military capability must be considered from an integrated perspective, optimised in the context of other available tools, be that of a diplomatic, economic, political, or even psychological nature.

Given that war has proven to be such a pivotal game changer, theories of how it best should be conducted dates back millennia. The Prussian general Carl von Clausewitz (1780–1831) is considered to be the proverbial father of modern warfare strategies. His work On War (Vom Krige) is still widely read and is part of the curriculum in many military academies. Remarkable, given that it now dates back almost two centuries, and with the technical upgrades we have seen, not unusually driven by armed conflicts themselves, which have made the way wars were fought in his days unrecognisable with how war is conducted today. On War is considered a difficult read; for one, it was posthumously compiled by his widow from a selection of Clausewitz's earlier writings, some just being unfinished drafts that reflected thoughts finding their form, and these were not conclusively arranged chronologically. But also, his complex writing style, in both the original German as well as the English translations, reflects a world view that in many aspects are vastly different to ours. Clausewitz was obviously influenced by the Enlightenment Era he lived in, where questioning perceived truths and dogma brought science forward considerably. Acting in that spirit, his writings were a break with the reigning theories on warfare, as his approach to strategy took its starting point in realism rather than an ivory tower perspective. He recognised that re-enacting historical battles and from these seeking to derive rules to replicate, which was for the time the prescribed manner to teach warfare, would not capture the many irrational moments that are bound to occur in a conflict, as being able to capitalise on these were often decisive for the outcome. In fact, these situations were rarely properly chronicled in the historical records which often gave a too idealised description of the events. According to Clausewitz, what defined military genius, was a combination of rational cognitive faculties and a creative capacity that often is described as intuition, which provided an ability to competently deal with the irrational moments where fixed rules cannot be indiscriminately applied. It is from this perspective Clausewitz's writings must be considered, and it was for its time revolutionary, as he argued that a war theory cannot be formulated in terms of strict operational guidelines. He instead suggested broad-brushed principles because armed conflicts could only be planned to a minor degree given this irrationality that would arise from a number of uncertainties, using the term frictions, of which some were:

- insufficient intelligence about the enemy
- rumours that, true or not, influence perceptions
- an unrealistic understanding of one's own military capacities
- miscalculation of allied troops' capabilities and intents
- a discrepancy between expectations of outcome and realities on the ground
- issues with supplies and logistics[1]

WHAT IS WAR REALLY?

One might argue that war is a bit like pornography, one knows it when one sees it, but defining it is no easy matter. Clausewitz provided a definition of the rationality of war, considering it being merely an instrument, and not serving a purpose itself: "war is nothing but a duel on a larger scale [and] an act of force to compel our enemy to do our will," and that physical force constitutes the means to "render the enemy powerless."[2]

Therefore, he argued that war should not be treated as a separate matter but has to be contextualised from a political perspective, and a war strategy has to be designed with political objectives in mind. In the current setting, one can somewhat further expand on Clausewitz's view of war as the capacity to use organised force for political purposes, regardless of it resulting in actual violence or not. Hence, what can be considered a credible threat of using violence might therefore already constitute war, of course this makes this definition of war much more void of bloodletting than previously thought of. This especially in the context of some nation's access to nuclear deterrents, which would classify the Cold War era as an actual war, where sabre rattling at times could give the desired political effect – the Cuban Missile Crisis in 1962 being a case in point, as well as the numerous proxy wars that were fought between the East and West by, outwardly at least, non-state-affiliated militias and even criminal groups. Thus, it could be argued that the current trade war between the US and China, if it eventually includes being backed by a credible threat of violence, under this definition also would be classified as war proper. Philosophical ponderings such as these make the definition of war a highly blurred exercise, and one is bound to occasionally land in the fringes of what commonly and traditionally has been understood as war, namely, organised violence of some magnitude that is acted out for a continuous period of time. It is also important to ascertain who the combatants are, they need not exclusively be interstate adversaries but could include domestic groups that seek political control of existing or perceived nations through engaging in coordinated fighting, not unusually overlapping with criminal activities. In all, a conservative core definition of war would then read as:

- organised violence
- waged by two or more distinguishable groups against each other

- in pursuit of some political objective (meaning power within a social construct)
- sufficiently large in scale and social impact to attract the attention of political leaders
- continuing over a period long enough for the interplay between the opponents to have impact on events[3]

By analysing war from a political narrative, Clausewitz introduced a key fundament that came to hold together much of his theories, something he referred to as *wunderliche Dreifaltigkeit* which translates to something like "the remarkable trinity." The three parts, which can also be viewed as points of attractions, are:

- passions (irrational forces), and in this context typically being hatred and animosity, Clausewitz attached them to the people
- probability and chance, which represented the military forces and their capacity for creativity on the battlefield
- rational calculations, being represented by the government (and one can only wonder if Clausewitz in our times would have bestowed governments with such competence)

These three forces can form a number of combinations, as they are interconnected, and will come to define the unique character of each armed conflict. In essence, they are a representation of the amalgamation of irrationality, random elements of chance, and reason, which together will influence the outcome of a battle. One of them might be dominating but they tend to be shifting over the course of a military campaign, and it is this ongoing dynamic interaction that is so decisive for the articulation of a war strategy. Thus, it becomes critical to understand the psychological makeup and intellectual abilities of an opponent as these are such influential components in Clausewitz's trinity, in particular the *modus operandi* military leaders apply when confronted with the unknown. It was this insight and the manner in which he articulated it in a simple yet elastic formula that covered both the motivational forces and execution capabilities in armed conflicts that came to set Clausewitz far apart from existing war theories, which were merely focused on static formations.[4]

So, drumming up passionate war fever in people through promoting jingoism, scapegoating, or similar tactics allows for the psychological backing of engaging in military campaigns; initially at least, a military genius of sorts is required to capitalise on any unexpected opportunities that are bound to arise on the battlefield with intuition playing an important part, and finally rational and realistic political objectives set by the government, in all the making of the optimal trinity combination. A war strategy, therefore, needs to be shaped by these calibrated considerations, not in a fixed setting but by being able to adjust as changes occur. Important to note is that the technical capacities of one's arsenal was not part of this trinity, and that was not for historical reasons, the development of new weaponry was notable during Clausewitz's years, this as both the constraints and objectives of politics decided much of the extent of its actual deployment.[5]

THERE IS WAR AND THEN THERE IS WAR...

To prove the point of irrationality distorting any perceived war logic, Clausewitz distinguished between war in its purest, or most extreme, form — *absolute war* — which is war not controlled by politics as it is allowed to roam freely with no holdbacks of firepower. An absolute war will in effect come to mean an elimination war which goes on until one side is literally wiped out. In stark contrast stands the *limited war*, which is the most common form where political considerations will influence, almost always moderating them, the objectives of military targets and also the overarching means to get there. Albeit tactical short-term objectives are typically left to the generals' discretion. Clausewitz spent considerable time to explore the differences between this idealised pure form of war with how it is fought in reality given the many practical constraints that always come to apply. They would only overlap if and when the political ambition was total annihilation of the enemy, with a *carte blanche* provided to the armed forces, something which only infrequently has happened historically. But, mostly, these frictions on the ground distorted the theoretical abstractions, with the outcome on the battlefield to a large degree decided by the level of competency of the military leadership to handle these.[6]

THE NONLINEAR FEATURES OF WAR

What Clausewitz was perhaps the first to do was to theorise the many elements of irrationality that are bound to occur in armed conflicts. These are acknowledged to be notoriously difficult to predict both in terms of content, magnitude, and timing. Previous war theories often assumed highly idealised cause–effect relationships, something which have made them mere paper products for armchair generals, impossible to practically apply. Referring to frictions, these general uncertainties originate from an armed conflict's occurrences of random events, confusion, mistakes, poor intelligence, exhaustion, delays, distractions, disobedience, unreliability, fear, and sufferings that simply time, space, and the character of human nature will inevitably produce. For anyone with a knowledge of mathematics in general and nonlinearity in particular will undoubtedly recognise Clausewitz's friction concept as they share similarities with the features of chaos theory, namely that differences in input, however miniscule, very quickly lead to vast, and even completely altered, outcomes. What he referred to was a mathematical phenomena labelled "sensitive dependence on initial conditions," or more commonly, simply chaos. Hence, from a chaos theory perspective, war can be described as having an inherently unknowable number of (mostly) unquantifiable variables, all of which may interact with one another in an unpredictable way. This makes any attempt to formulate a mathematical equation of war largely indeterminable, making it difficult to be analytically predicted with any degree of precision. Proportionality or additivity will therefore not apply in the nonlinear setting of war, which is instead highlighted by erratic behaviour through the high likelihood of disproportionality in any direction.

That said, it does not mean that war as a whole is entirely random, it can be broken down in parts, of which some contain little random elements and therefore can be planned with high precision. Near-term situations can often be relatively well forecasted by an experienced military leadership, and in these situations cause–effect relationships apply quite well, especially if there is a noted superiority in military resources and technology which will clearly tilt the probability of outcome. However, for most parts, frictions will appear highlighted by nonlinear features, such as when a change of sorts suddenly crosses a threshold, which usually is not previously known, it triggers a regime shift (a statistical term) causing a drastic change of conditions to which previous parameters no longer apply. An arbitrarily small change could therefore generate an entirely different trajectory, and anecdotally there are many stories of how battles have been won in such ways.

Probably unknowingly, Clausewitz described accurately the characteristics of the inherent unpredictability of a chaotic environment, recognising that it is not possible to know in advance what feature will trigger the commotions that can lead to catastrophic outcomes. Thus, the acknowledgement of chaos explains why Clausewitz refrained from providing much detailed tactical advice; it was simply not possible to do so in any generic terms. Hence, he suggested that an insightful and victorious commander therefore is the one that can recognise which frictions hold the propensity for drastic change and is agile enough to use them in one's favour. He was also to the point in the understanding that historical explanations of battles had to be cautiously interpreted, as the decisive factors or chain of events being the true root causes were so subtle and intricate that it is likely that they were never fully understood by neither eyewitness nor later historians, and it would explain why historical events are so frequently reinterpreted as discourses change over time. There was also the realisation that conscious actions will inevitably often have unintended consequences and it is not unusual that actions taken of seemingly great importance produces little, and acts of apparently miniscule standing have, on occasion, colossal impacts.[7]

SO, WAS CLAUSEWITZ COMPLETELY SILENT ON ANY PRACTICAL ADVICE ON HOW TO ACTUALLY WAGE WAR?

Given Clausewitz's dynamic view on warfare, by necessity, the number of universal principles that he could provide were going to be few, such as the remarkable trinity, and hence might explain their longevity until current times; however. their broad-brushed flexibility has also been one of the main critiques against them. But, beyond these he did provide some more hard-and-fast practical guidance on how to actually wage war? In selecting military objectives, Clausewitz introduced the idea of identifying the enemy's Schwerpunkt, which is usually translated as centre of gravity (COG), but can also be read as weight of effort. In essence, it is the point to concentrate one's military efforts against, not necessarily the weakest spot in the defence line but the insertion point that would provide the quickest path for a breakthrough towards victory. He gave some examples of what that could be: in a country where rivalling groups are fighting for control, it would usually be the capital, and in popular uprisings, the schwerpunkt would be the personality of its leaders and public opinion. In the Second World War, Adolf Hitler was probably the schwerpunkt that the Allied should have attacked to quickly end the war, and it is surprising that not more attempts to end his life were orchestrated by them. Thus, it could have both physical and psychological targets. The document outlining the boundaries and direction of the schwerpunkt was the Aufmarschanweisungen (deployment instructions). Once identified, it would be against a schwerpunkt that the (military) energies are directed. Attacking it provided the best opportunity to achieve final victory through directing an operational approach to establish a schwerpunktlinie, described as the shortest and most direct distance between one's own base of operations and the schwerpunkt. Of course, by concentrating the efforts on an identified schwerpunkt meant that troops had to be reduced in other sectors, opening up for one's own schwerpunkts that the enemy could consider for attack [8]

Clausewitz also discussed the offense–defence dichotomy. He argued that defence is the stronger form of warfare, as it only has a negative objective, seeking nothing beyond self-preservation. Whilst the attacker always has the advantage of initiative, and the timing thereof, with the typical objectives of increasing his geographical, economic, or political strength through conquest, Clausewitz still considered it the weaker form of warfare. Why was it so? Important for him were the operational and strategic aspects of defence, however strongly an offensive attack may start out, it tends to weaken as it advances from its original base due to running out of resources and problems with providing adequate supply fast enough. Moreover, public opinion and the balance-of-power equation are more likely to favour the defender. The essence of a prudent defence strategy rests on the ability to wait: until the plans of the enemy have been ascertained and understood, until the military strength has tilted to one's favour, or for any improvement in the defender's situation, whether from the attacker reaching a culminating point due to supply problems or battle fatigue, or from outside intervention, or from mobilisation of his own resources, or from some chance development that can be advantageously used. But as the defender always cedes the initiative to the opponent, he can therefore not seek to gain anything tangible but time, hoping for the opportunity to counterattack or use some other means that weakens the enemy's desire to attack. Important to note is that with waiting, Clausewitz did not imply mere passivity, an effective defence must be profoundly active, it should be "a shield made up of well-directed blows." This, as it at some point must be able to shift to an offensive strategy, and it was this dynamic timing between these two that Clausewitz reflected upon.[9]

CLAUSEWITZ'S LEGACY

On War has been interpreted in many ways, both theoretically and how it was practically implemented on the battlefield, something which is not strange given the more principle-like strategy rather than detailed operational advice it promoted. Most agree though that the gist of Clausewitz's writings lies in describing the random features of war, where psychology plays an important role, and the combatant nimble and resilient enough to understand and leverage the unforeseen is likely to be the one coming out victorious.

One of the practical applications, at least in parts, of Clausewitz's theories was the famous German Second World War tactic *blitzkrieg*, which can be translated as "lightning war." Whilst the origin of the word is somewhat unclear, its deployment was pretty straightforward, albeit for the time unconventional. It evolved from German experiences in the First World War on the Eastern front, which, unlike the Western front that was locked down in trench warfare, was characterised by the more traditional free-flowing military campaigns and battles. Studies after the war highlighted that size was not decisive but that a smaller highly coordinated unit could have more combat power than a larger slow-moving force. Speed was an important factor as through ensuring superior mobility and faster decision-making, adaptable and motorised units could act quicker than the forces opposing them.[10]

These insights formed the edifice of the blitzkrieg tactics which was a mixing and matching of armed capabilities seeking to optimise and concentrate military force, often against a superior opponent. This was achieved by finding the opportunity to break through a weak point in the defence line, the aforementioned *schwerpunkt*, thereby seeking to achieve a victory quickly and decisively. The element of surprise played an important role in creating a sensation of shock which would help to break the enemy's will to fight. Thus, the psychological impact was vital in whether such an audacious venture would be successful. It was the combination of mobilised infantry, tanks, artillery, and aircrafts operating in a highly coordinated manner seeking to create a focussed overwhelming power to deliver a knockout blow through surprise, before the enemy would have a chance to regroup and consolidate their forces, that was the kernel of a blitzkrieg attack. The blitzkrieg tactics also influenced the chain of command structure, where delegation of initiative was promoted amongst junior officers; hence attacks were often issued without detailed and explicit orders, this to allow for circumventing any frictions that inevitably would arise. The intent of the attack was what typically was communicated by the military headquarter command down the ranks, with unit leaders allowed to, in a discretionary manner, interpret and apply means to meet the objectives in the midst of fighting. This enabled much higher speed in execution in contrast to strict hierarchical command chains, where also minutiae needed approval before they could be acted upon. The ethos of blitzkrieg was "the higher the authority, the more general the orders," leaving it to the lower echelons to fill in the details.[11,12]

Blitzkrieg tactics relied on certain factors to be successful, given the very nature of its operations, speed, and combining forces deeply penetrating the front and seeking to capture objectives far behind enemy lines required favourable terrain, flat land to keep the speed high and easy access for tanks and mechanised infantry. It needed air superiority to integrate attacks from the air force with the ground forces' forward movements requiring the weather to be on their side, it meant clear skies. Surprise and employing psychological methods were important to create disarray, causing the enemy into panic when attacked by full force especially in areas where an attack was not expected. This reduced the risk for a counterattack or the risk of the enemy quickly regrouping. But there was also an inherent weakness in the very foundation of blitzkrieg tactics, namely its speed, which came to hamper its success rate. After a breakthrough through enemy lines, they have to quickly force them to surrender, as the speed in which the attack moved made it hard to follow up with ample reserves and supplies on time. This was pivotal to ensure that momentum could be kept, not causing voids and disconnects that could be closed by an adaptable opponent willing to sacrifice territory for a chance to regroup into more viable positions, something which came to hamper the German advance into the Soviet Union as part of Operation Barbarossa in 1941. Overextending supply lines was a major risk for blitzkrieg.

Several war strategists have accused both Clausewitz's theories and the practical adoption of blitzkrieg of not really qualifying as doctrines proper as they view them as lacking coherent theories and being so elastic that they can be interpreted in far too many ways to form a distinct standard. However, their *ad hoc*-ness is what made them viable, this by at all times applying the pragmatical view on how to overcome problems and allowing for decisions to be made at the ground level rather than in a strict top-down manner. In that sense, the critiques they have been right as blitzkrieg describes more the means of arranging and utilising military forces in the best way possible to increase the likelihood for the desired outcome, namely victory achieved in a rapid and surprise manner.[13]

As time has progressed, weapons have become more advanced and deadlier to the point one can only assume was unfathomable in Clausewitz's time. With the advent and deployment of the atomic bomb in 1945, only two decades later there was already a capacity to annihilate the whole world, if the US and the Soviet Union actually had decided to engage in an all-out conflict. That insight made them abstain from a full-scale war, and interestingly enough from the Second World War onwards, the number of casualties from war has come down significantly. A case in point is the *Battle of the Somme* in the First World War, which counted deaths to over 1 million in a 5-months-long battle involving a total of more than 5.5 million men, in contrast to *Operation Desert Storm* in 1991, where the US coalition had amassed almost 1 million men and only saw 292 casualties. This remarkable trend is perhaps more due to accurate precision weapons that can strike without much collateral damage not having to involve large troop commitments on any side. There is also now a high political price to pay for too large a number of deaths, especially after the Vietnam War, not only one's own troops but also on the enemy side. War nowadays tends to engage far fewer combatants; despite the increase in world population since the First World War, sizes of armed forces have shrunk considerably. Instead there is now a greater reliance on special forces that are able to, with small teams, strike particular targets, considered especially vulnerable for an enemy, mini *schwerpunkts* of sorts. Non-lethal combat methods and the deployment of psychological warfare are increasingly being used, trying to break the enemy's will to fight rather than to outright get rid of them. War has morphed into new formats where the size of military units and the capacity of the military arsenal, bombs and bullets, no longer are the sole decisive factors for the outcome of a battle, rather seeking to precisely strike at perceived *schwerpunkts*, often of an abstract nature, have become the preferred mean of warfare.

As much as the way war is conducted has evolved, is it possible to define an evolutionary path of warfare versus the theories of Clausewitz? One way of describing the evolvement of war is the generational approach, currently counting four generations, some argue five, and whilst far from being universally adopted, it does provide a fair illustration of some of the most important changing features of warfare over the last centuries.

The first-generation warfare started to form after the *Peace of Westphalia* in 1648 ending the *Thirty Years' War* when newly minted states needed a structure to organise their armed forces for future wars. It was strict top-down command and control, where troops were arranged to fight in close formations, such as line and column tactics. It sought to bring a linear order to the battlefields, and wars often took the form of head-to-head collisions and outflanking tactics between such opposing formations. Military forces were synchronised through standardised uniforms, a formalised officer hierarchy, and disciplined military drill. In short, it introduced a more systematic way of waging war.

The transition to a second generation was a response to the technological developments, as swords and shields and bows and arrows were being replaced by automatic rifles and long-range artillery. Marching long lines of men in straight formations against barrages of machine gun fire turned into massacres. By the First World War, the new technological developments forced a change to military thinking and a second-generation warfare strategy emerged. Disciplined formations became less common and to break the trench warfare stalemate, concentrated artillery and pitched battle arrangement were deployed. Second-generation warfare still maintained lines of battle but established smaller units of men to allow for more mobile manoeuvring, German *Stormtroopers* were introduced to this effect. These smaller units allowed for faster advances and the ability to use cover and concealment to their advantage. Infiltration rather than meeting the enemy head on became a preferred tactic. Linearity on the battlefield was starting to dissipate.

The second generation transcended into the third generation of modern warfare with, amongst others, the blitzkrieg tactics, where coordination between units was enabled through radio communications, highlighting the superiority of speed and stealth over static positions. The Second World War came to be the end point of linear warfare with surprise outmanoeuvring taking precedent, often seeking to strike deep at the enemy's rear. Of course, this meant drastic changes to the traditional military hierarchy: junior officers became more empowered to make decisions in the spur of the moment and the role of headquarter command instead focused on coordination and strategy. Strict regimental doctrine started to break down. With improvements in transportation, parachute drops and helicopters became pivotal instruments in facilitating the element of surprise. Special forces became an integral part of most armed forces. These third-generation tactics have very much remained an integrated form of warfare and explain why the armed forces of today are, in terms of manpower, so much smaller than those of the last century. And of course, with the advent of missiles and long-range bombers, technology could in parts completely replace troop deployment.[14,15]

The fourth-generation warfare originated from the Cold War era, where proxy wars and use of non-state combatants became prevalent as a direct nuclear confrontation could have led to a complete wipe-out of both sides, and in effect became a political impossibility. Paradoxical, as the weapons became more advanced and lethal, and there was instead a more distinct focus on "hearts and mind" campaigns seeking to win over the population in contested areas, including a heavy emphasis on psychological warfare and the establishment of liberation movements or insurgent groups. The fourth generation has come to blur the boundaries between war and politics, and between soldiers and civilians. Nation states have lost a lot of their monopoly on violence, private groups can, like pre-first generation buccaneers, again play pivotal roles in conflict and conflict generation. A fourth-generation war typically includes the following features:

- Politically complex
- use of insurgency tactics, such as subversion, terrorism and guer-rilla tactics, striking at soft targets, often being an attack on an opponent's cultural or societal narrative
- combatants are organised through a highly decentralised struc-ture with a lack of hierarchy, small in size, spread out networks of communication and financial support
- psychological warfare plays a major role
- military efforts are integrated with political, economic, and social tools used in hybrid warfare
- low-intensity conflicts where the treatment of non-combatants becomes tactical dilemmas

Hence, combatants in a fourth-generation war have the following characteristics: lack of hierarchical authority, lack of formal struc-ture, equipped with patience and flexibility, an ability to keep a low profile when needed, and being of small size and of a (relatively) low cost effort. Fourth-generation warfare takes place in all spheres: economic, political, media, military, and civilian and forces conven-tional military units to adapt their tactics to fight in a corresponding manner. [16,17]

Wars are now fought on multidimensional levels, transcending far beyond mere physical violence, often focussed on deploying methods of non-violence. Gandhi was perhaps one of the first to prove the might of meeting violence with non-violent means, by de-escalating whilst the British colonial authorities were escalating. He thereby targeted the collective psychology seeking to gain the upper moral high ground by making the enemy appear as a bully-ing tyrant, who subsequently lost support both internationally and nationally. For a fourth-generation combatant taking on government forces, to win at the battlefield is often a physical impossibility as their arsenal cannot outmatch that of a state-led opponent. Instead they must psychologically convince their adversaries that their goals of eliminating them are either unachievable or too costly for the perceived benefits, thus by merely focusing on survival, it is possible to change the reigning discourse, whether that be of political ideology, nationalism, or religion. Therefore, in these wars, the *schwerpunkt* is typically an abstract rather than a physical location or target. Hence, the only way for state-led armed forces to beat such an opponent with both fluid and resilient characteristics is by realising that their *schwerpunkt* is their political leadership and/or trying to dominate the psychological narrative through psychological warfare. The crafting of a warfare strategy in a fourth-generation setting needs to involve a hybrid perspective, including an amalgamation of tools and an insightful understanding on how these influence each other in order to optimise their consolidated powers.

One of the first attempts to theoretically articulate this type of fourth-generation warfare (whilst not labelled as such) saw its genesis in the de-colonialisation era in Africa, Asia, and the Middle East. In Algeria, the French army had to drastically adapt its tactics to take on the FLN guerrilla. The French colonel Roger Trinquier (1908–1986) published what was one of the first works on counterinsurgency techniques, tactics which successfully were put to test at the *Battle of Algiers* in 1956–1957 when the local FLN group was eliminated. His book *Modern Warfare: A French View of Counterinsurgency* from 1961 has since become a classic and was in part implemented by the Portuguese in their colonial wars where they successfully managed to combat clandestine enemies on three fronts. Trinquier defined this form of war as follows:

> Warfare is now an interlocking system of actions political, economic, psychological, military—that aims at the overthrow of the established authority in a country and its replacement by another regime. To achieve this end, the aggressor tries to exploit the internal tensions of the country attacked—ideological, social, religious, economic —any conflict liable to have a profound influence on the population to be conquered.[18]

Trinquier acknowledged that unlike previous eras, modern warfare is generally not officially declared permitting the adversary to continue to take advantage of peacetime legislation, and to pursue their activities both covertly and openly. An enemy will thereby strive by every means to preserve the fiction of peace. Therefore, the surest means of unveiling a fourth-generation, guerrilla-type movement is to declare a state of war at the earliest moment, or at least at the very latest when the first symptoms of the struggle are revealed in political assassinations, terrorism, guerrilla activities, etc. Thus, obtaining timely information becomes a vital part, and Trinquier has been heavily criticised for endorsing torture as part of counterinsurgency techniques but he defended these practices as one of the key success factors in the Battle of Algiers, arguing that information is nothing in itself, particularly during a crisis, if it is not quickly exploited.[19] Over time, the reliance on information has only increased, required for many deceptive operations to psychologically gain influence over an enemy, and that is what Chapter 2 will deal with (Figure 1.1).

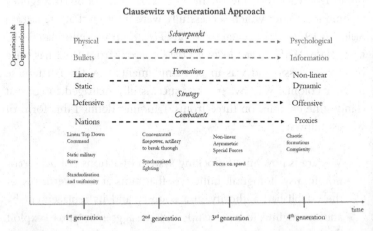

Figure 1.1 A schematic overview of the generational warfare approach versus key Clausewitzian concepts.

NOTES

1 von Clausewitz, Carl. On War ([Vom Kriege] Editor and translator Howard, Michael, Paret, Peter. Princeton, NJ: Princeton University Press, (1989) [1832]).

2 Ibid.

3 Bassford, Christopher. Policy, Politics, War, and Military Strategy (The Clausewitz Homepage, 1997–2015). http://www.clausewitz.com/readings/Bassford/StrategyDraft/index.htm (accessed 1 January 2021).

4 von Clausewitz, Carl. On War ([Vom Kriege] Editor and translator Howard, Michael, Paret, Peter. Princeton, NJ: Princeton University Press, (1989) [1832]).

5 Ibid.

6 Ibid.

7 Beyerchen, Alan D. Clausewitz, Nonlinearity and the Unpredictability of War (International Security, Vol. 17, Issue 3 (Winter, 1992–1993)). pp. 59–90.

8 von Clausewitz, Carl. OnWar ([Vom Kriege] Editor and translator Howard, Michael, Paret, Peter. Princeton, NJ: Princeton University Press, (1989) [1832]).

9 Ibid.

10 Corum, James S. The Roots of Blitzkrieg: Hans von Seeckt and German Military Reform (Modern War Studies. Lawrence: University Press of Kansas, 1992).

11 Frieser, Karl-Heinz. The Blitzkrieg Legend: The 1940 Campaign in the West ([Blitzkrieg-legende: der westfeldzug 1940] trans. J. T. Greenwood. Annapolis, MD: Naval Institute Press, 2005).

12 Citino, Robert M. The German Way of War: From the Thirty Years'War to the Third Reich (Lawrence: University of Kansas Press, 2005).

13 Naveh, Shimon. In Pursuit of Military Excellence: The Evolution of Operational Theory (London: Frank Cass, 1997).

14 Lind, William S., Nightengale, Keith, Schmitt, John F., Sutton, Joseph W., Wilson, Gary I. The Changing Face of War: Into the Fourth Generation (Marine Corps Gazette, October 1989). pp. 22–26.

15 Lind, William S. Understanding Fourth Generation War (15 January 2004). www.antiwar.com (accessed 1 January 2021).

16 Thornton, Rod. Asymmetric Warfare (Malden, MA: Polity Press, 2007).

17 Vest, Jason. Fourth-Generation Warfare (The Atlantic, 01 December 2001).

18 Trinquier, Roger. *Modern Warfare: A French View of Counterinsurgency* (Leavenworth, KS: Army University Press, 1961). https://www.armyupress.army.mil/Portals/7/combat-studies-institute/csi-books/Modern-Warfare.pdf (accessed 1 January 2021).

19 Ibid.

2

WELCOME TO THE MURKY WORLD OF PSYCHOLOGICAL WARFARE

Der ganze Krieg setzt menschliche Schwäche voraus, und gegen sie ist er gerichtet.

All war presupposes human weakness and seeks to exploit it.

Carl von Clausewitz (1780–1831)
legendary German war strategist

Beyond Clausewitz, Sun Tzu is often the only other military theorist of notoriety that laymen are familiar with. A highly mythical figure, and if he at all existed was a Chinese general (est 544 BC–est 496 BC). Sun Tzu is often referred to when highlighting the earliest known writings of what today is commonly referred to as psychological warfare. His *The Art of War* is in particular known through its insightful aphorisms that are still widely quoted, perhaps more amongst management consultants than in military circles, to the point of being worn out. However, as useful as certain of these individual aphorisms are, his book overall lacks Clausewitz's profound coherency from the strategical perspective. Sun Tzu is sometimes contrasted against Clausewitz's more physical battle strategies, as he formulated numerous ways of tricking and conjuring the enemy to give up without actually engaging in head on battle. However, this dichotomy is flimsy as both shared the view that destroying the enemy's will rather than himself is what a strategy should focus on. And a reader of Clausewitz's work cannot but notice the importance he did put on the influence psychology had on the outcome of war, including from firing up the masses and infusing them with war fever to how a capable military commander should be able to handle stress and uncertainties. Attempting to influence psychological perspectives in war has of course been going on since the earliest days of mankind, but it was really only during the Second World War that it became more formalised and structured as standalone military units, and its usage has been accentuated ever since. As psychological warfare has evolved over time, with its tools becoming more defined and refined, the vocabulary has also changed, at times causing confusion as these terms are used interchangeably with somewhat differing definitions. It was previously referred to as political warfare but psychological warfare can extend beyond the purely political perspective to also target other aspects. More recently, psychological warfare has been compared to marketing campaigns, given the many, superficially at least, shared techniques such as impacting attitudes, strategic influence, and perception management. *Hearts and minds* campaigns perhaps more poetically describe what it is all about, attempting through various means with both emotional and rational arguments to convince an enemy that resistance is futile and trying to win them over to one's side. An older highbrow definition of psychological warfare reads "to denote any action which is practiced mainly by psychological methods with the aim of evoking a planned psychological reaction in other people."[1,2]

IN PSYCHOLOGICAL WARFARE, SWORD AND SHIELD ARE INFORMATION AND CREDIBILITY

In perhaps a somewhat condescending way, propaganda is the crude term to describe the main instrument of psychological warfare, the use of information, however truthful, seeking to change existing perceptions of reality towards a worldview that embraces the originator's ulterior objectives. Hence, information, in its many variations, is the key fundament of psychological warfare and therefore it has often been branded as information warfare. However, as technology has advanced so significantly after the Second World War, information warfare has emerged to include many other aspects, and psychological warfare is now considered to be a subset thereof. Broadly, information warfare covers

- espionage and intelligence, which include everything from hacking to cracking passwords
- sabotage, including viruses, denial of service attacks, and similar
- defensive strategies to maintain the integrity of information platforms through various means of electronic protection, including anti-virus software
- deception, which largely equates with psychological warfare, which is the focus of this chapter

Psychological warfare operations can be broadly divided into three categories:

1 **White propaganda.** sticking to objective truths that as far as possible refrain from bias, with the sources of information being fully acknowledged
2 **Grey propaganda.** broadly truthful statements or those with elements of truths that contain no information that can be proven wrong. Sources typically not disclosed
3 **Black propaganda.** falsifications and deceitful information provided being attributed to false sources[3]

The differentiation of propaganda categories highlights the key foundation of psychological warfare, *credibility*. For a propaganda campaign to be viewed as plausible, its recipients must acknowledge, implicitly at least, the source as credible, as otherwise its message will be rejected, and can in fact trigger an adverse effect of taking the opposite view of what is being touted. Hence, to be viewed as credible becomes a determinant of whether the instruments of psychological warfare are successful or not; only rarely do exceptions apply from this rule. Some argue that credibility is a condition of persuasion; in essence, before you can make an individual do as you say, you must make him believe what you say.[4] Credibility towards the targeted audiences, but also towards other media resources, is something described as difficult to obtain but easy to lose. And there is a noted contradiction between the ambition of wanting to quickly achieve results and the arduous work with building credibility. The temptation is always there to use grey or black propaganda, where the source is deliberately erroneous when a fast response is required, as it can provide a short-term victory or relief, but will ruin the successful prospects of longer-term engagements. Hence, grey and black operations come with great risk, as sooner or later groups that are being exposed to the propaganda will come to see through the untruths they contain, with the originators and sources being discredited as false and unreliable. So, any mixing and matching of propaganda categories from the same originator will hence dilute also true statements, being considered as half-truths, or even outright lies, once the targeted audience has identified discrepancies, or the originator is not viewed as trustworthy from the onset. For governments seeking the moral high ground in conflicts, they will be confined to stick to white propaganda to maintain their integrity toward their citizens and other nations. This insight has become something of a golden rule to which most governmental agencies in democracies nowadays adhere to, namely only white propaganda is allowed, meaning that both the information and the source are objectively verified and clearly stated. For instance, historians have shown that most of the Allied propaganda in the Second World War could be classified as white propaganda. This can create an asymmetric relationship in a conflict between combatants such as government forces and insurgents. David Galula, in his book *Counterinsurgency Warfare* (1964, 2006), highlights this asymmetry in the usage of information: the insurgent, having no civic responsibility, is free to use every trick; if necessary, he can lie, cheat, and exaggerate. He is not obliged to prove any of his claims and he is usually judged by what he promises and not by what he does. Consequently, grey or black propaganda will be a powerful information weapon to him, something which he is aware a government cannot use as freely, or more likely not at all. This creates an asymmetric advantage as they will not be held accountable in the same way as their government opponent who are tied to codes of conducts, international conventions, and the discharge of state responsibilities. It has only proven possible to deploy grey and black propaganda in authoritarian regimes, where no political opposition can disprove statements and uncover deceptions; however, most of the population would already be (highly) sceptical to any government statements anyhow. But for a legitimate regime, the objective of psychological warfare must be to inform rather than deceive. This asymmetry in how information is managed and organised will in the short term, at least, favour the insurgent, which can use it to its advantage to be proactive with issuing negative statements and degrading propaganda, forcing the defender into a reactive mode, at all times seeking to debunk accusations, mostly having to focus on responding and reacting to what is likely to be false statements with the insurgent hoping that at least something of its propaganda will stick.

David Kilcullen, in his book from 2009 *Accidental Guerrilla*, describes the emphasis that insurgents put on information, including its handling and circulation. The insurgents treat propaganda as their main device, often deliberately coordinating physical attacks to augment a sophisticated propaganda campaign.[5] The requirements for a government, in psychological warfare campaigns, to stick to the truth at all times can become a bottleneck and a vulnerability, as they need to do proper fact checks until a message can be released. This time delay in response is often of vital importance, as valuable momentum is lost, and it is typically the first and false dispatch that sticks in the collective mind. A delayed response often does not hit the top headlines and tends to be forgotten. But as governments are bound by legal, political, and hierarchical bureaucratic structures, they are often rejected the opportunity to respond with decisive speed.[6]

SOME KNOWN TACTICS DEPLOYED IN PSYCHOLOGICAL WARFARE

Psychological warfare seeks to change behaviour, it either aspires to get an adversary to go from active to passive mode: in the most typical scenario to cease aggressions or, more challenging, reverse the aggression towards their own leadership instead. One can broadly distinguish between two time frames, the one-off short-term where the propagandist is seeking an imminent emotional response, such as that of shock, where deception and outright lies are often deployed to create sensation. The other is the long-term campaign aspiring to alter, often permanently, the target audience's narrative. The former is a tactic more likely to be successful, however short lived, whilst the later takes considerable effort and time to prove rewarding.

The design of propaganda should, much like a marketing slogan, follow four basic criteria; it must be seen, understood, remembered, and acted on.[7] A propagandist needs to fully understand the target audience in that being aligned with its existing opinions, beliefs, and dispositions to craft messages that creates the desired resonance. To this point, the French philosopher and sociologist Jacques Ellul (1912–1994), who has written some of the most influential works on propaganda, is quoted:

> The propagandist builds his techniques on the basis of his knowledge of man, his tendencies, his desires, his needs, his psychic mechanisms, his conditioning.[8]

So, rather than try to change political loyalties, ethnic or religious attitudes, or other deeply held beliefs, the propagandist seeks to align his feelings about these things with those of the target group, making messages appearing to be resonant, such as to be coming from within the audience rather than from the outside. Messages that are supportive of, rather than discrepant from, commonly held views are more likely to be effective. Propagandists, like marketing managers, develop their campaigns on the biological insights that humans through herding instincts tend to make decision as part of groups, and that emotions, particularly if one is able to induce strong ones such as anger and fear, will distort and tend to override rational arguments. Research on group behaviour has shown that people will go along with the group even when the group makes decisions contrary to privately held beliefs and values. These conforming tendencies are what a propagandist will seek to exploit.[9,10]

Psychological warfare campaigns deploy long-known techniques of conjuring and manipulation, some dating back to writings on rhetoric from the ancient Greeks, and are in that sense timeless, and these are also widely used in marketing, to influence behaviour of the intended recipients, many aspiring to trigger an immediate emotional reaction. In its most basic design, it either seeks to unite or divide its target audience, as described in Figure 2.1. Some of the most common propaganda techniques include the following:

- **Selective omission**, or cherry picking, is probably the most common technique, which is a process of choosing from a variety of facts only those that most effectively strengthen and authenticate the propagandist's objective. It includes the collection of available material pertaining to a subject and the selection of that material which most effectively supports the preferred view. It is structured in two

THE UNITE & DIVIDE PARADIGM

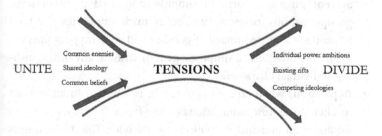

Figure 2.1 The Unite & Divide Paradigm that forms the foundation for most psychological warfare operations.

main phases: first the careful selection of favourable facts, presented to the target audience to obtain a desired reaction, and second the propagandist uses these facts as a basis for conclusions, trying to guide the audience into accepting the conclusions by acknowledging the facts presented. Essentially, this is framing of a narrative.

- **Simplification.** This is a technique in which the many facts of a situation are reduced so the right or wrong, good or evil, of an act or decision is obvious to all. It provides the simple black-and-white solution for complex problems; the big lie is a classic type of simplification. Statements are positive and firm; qualifying words are never used. It has the following characteristics:
  - It aspires to think for others: some accept information which they cannot verify personally as long as the source is acceptable to them, or the informant is considered an expert. Others absorb whatever they read, see, or hear with little or no discrimination, as they are simply too lazy or unconcerned to adequately think problems through, and others are uneducated and willingly accept convenient simplifications.
  - It is concise as simplification gives the impression of going to the heart of the matter in a few words.
  - It builds ego: some are reluctant to believe that any field of endeavour, except their own, is difficult to understand. Simplifications reinforce the ego of such individuals. It is what they would like to believe, because they are afraid that the subject in question may actually be beyond their capacity to understand.
- **Stereotyping** is a form of simplification used to fit persons, groups, nations, or events into ready-made categories that tend to produce a desired image of good or bad. Stereotyping puts the subject or event into a simplistic pattern without any distinguishing individual characteristics.
- **Repetition**, when an idea or position is repeated in an attempt to elicit an almost automatic response from the audience, or to reinforce an audience's opinions or attitudes. This technique is extremely valid and useful because human beings are basically creatures of habit and develop skills and values by repetition.[11]

As previously highlighted, credibility is the foundation upon which any successful propaganda rests, so to establish oneself as a credible source is a key undertaking for any propagandist. So, most propaganda broadcasts include an appeal to authority, even if sometimes only subtly, which cites prominent experts to support an argument or course of action through their knowledge and direction. To qualify as an expert in a specific topic, one needs typically to cover four characteristics:

1 **Accomplishment.** People have confidence in an authority who has demonstrated outstanding ability and proficiency in his field. This accomplishment should be related to the subject of the testimonial.
2 **Identification with the target.** People have greater confidence in an authority with whom they have a common bond.
3 **Position of authority.** An official position of authority may instil confidence in the testimony.
4 **Inanimate objects.** A device to transfer physical attributes of an inanimate object to the message, a monument such as the national flag or religious symbols, can serve as inanimate objects representing authority.[12]

Expert opinion is an effective tool in establishing a legitimacy of altering views and it often has an expanding effect, as once a source is accepted as an authority on one topic, another related topic may be established as well, founded on prior acceptance of the expertise. It becomes an important task for the propagandist to ascertain the audience's perceived image of the expert. Are they deferential and accept the message on the basis of thought leadership alone or is it met with scepticism and rejection? Hence, to achieve credibility, the propaganda-set-up arrangements must be carefully crafted to avoid any rejection or ridicule from the target audience. The source must have the authority to endorse the message which should include catch phrase slogans, ideally self-perpetuating often with elements of implicit stereotyping. Virtue words that target norms and values and produce a positive image when attached to a person or issue should be included, such as references to peace, happiness, security, wise leadership, freedom, and similar platitudes. Testimonials is another important device which may include quotations cited to support or reject a given policy, action, program, or personality. This is done in an effort to cause the target audience to identify itself with the authority and to accept the authority's opinions and beliefs as its own. These could be of an official sanction type, an endorsement of an authority as having approved the attributed idea, concept, action, or belief.

Once creditability has been established, a number of common propaganda strategies can be employed to promote the desired messages:

- **Assertions.** Assertions are positive statements presented as fact. They imply that what is stated is self-evident and needs no further proof. Assertions may or may not be true, hence can be part of white, grey, or black propaganda.
- **Bandwagon and the Inevitable Victory.** This technique attempts to persuade the target audience to take a course of action that "everyone else is taking." It reinforces people's natural desire to both join a crowd and be on the winning side. Inevitable victory invites those not already on the bandwagon to join and those already, or partially, on the bandwagon are being reassured that staying aboard is the best course of action.
- **Glorious Generalities.** By appealing to emotions such as love of country, family, or home, or the desire for peace, freedom, glory, and honour, the propagandists seek to gain approval for their messages without a deliberate examination of the actual reasons. However, the emotions aroused must be so intensely appealing and linked to highly held beliefs and values that they themselves are able to carry convictions without supporting information or reason. The glorious generalities themselves are typically often vague, meaning different things to different people, but they must overall hold a favourable connotation, appearing good and virtuous.

- **Identifying with the Common Man.** This approach attempts to convince the target audience that the propagandist's positions reflect the common sense of the people. It is designed to win the confidence by communicating in the common manner and style of the audience.
- **Incredible Truths.** A high-risk propaganda technique to be utilised when an immediate emotional response is needed, and this should only be used at specific occasions, such as
  - When the propagandist is certain that a vitally important event will take place.
  - An adverse event, even disastrous, or one of significant tactical or strategic importance, unfavourable to the enemy has occurred and the news has been hidden from the enemy public or troops.
  - The enemy government has denied or glossed over an event detrimental to its cause.

    For a propagandist, to broadcast an incredible truth can come with a double whammy effect; it will increase the credibility of the propagandist and simultaneously decrease the credibility of the enemy. Though such news will appear incredible, hence the label, to the enemy public, it is given full promotion by the propagandist to create shock and sensation. This as the event and its significance will eventually become known to the target audience in spite of the adversary's government efforts to hide it. The prime requirement in using this technique is that the disseminated incredible truth must be certain to become a reality, in that sense being white propaganda.
- **Insinuations.** A devious technique designed to create or stir up the suspicions of the target audience against ideas, groups, or individuals in order to divide an enemy. The propagandist hints, suggests, or implies, thereby allowing the audience to draw its own conclusions. Guilt by association is commonly used. Latent suspicions are exploited as attempts to structure them into active expressions of disunity which can weaken the enemy's war efforts. These exploitable vulnerabilities typically include political

differences within the targeted group and economic, ethnical, religious, or social differences. It could also target animosity towards the ruling elite or party, an attack on the tax system, a burdensome bureaucracy, inequalities between regions, or simply recognising the powerlessness of the individual vis-à-vis the government. There are a number of devices to facilitate insinuations:

- **Leading questions**, where the propagandist asks questions each of which has only one possible answer, obviously to the disadvantage for the adversary. In a military situation, it typically seeks to guide the opponents towards surrender or desertion as the only viable alternative to being annihilated by a seemingly superior combatant.

- **Humour** can be another form of insinuation, where jokes and cartoons about the enemy find a ready audience among those in the population who normally reject straightforward accusations or assertions. Jokes about totalitarian leaders and their subordinates have a noted tendency to spread with ease and rapidity amongst its citizens and can undermine their authority.

- **Pure motives**. This technique makes it clear that the side represented by the propagandist is acting in the best interests of the target audience, insinuating that the enemy is acting to the contrary.

- **Guilt by association**, which links a person, group, or idea to other persons, groups, or ideas held in contempt by the target audience. The insinuation rests on the accusation that the connection is not accidental.

- **Least of Evils.** Framing a course of action being taken as perhaps undesirable but that any alternative would result in an outcome far worse. Projecting blame on the enemy for the unpleasant or restrictive conditions is usually coupled with this technique.

- **Rationalisation.** Closely linked to generalities and vagueness, where these are utilised to rationalise acts or beliefs considered questionable by the reigning discourse.

- **Scapegoating.** This technique attempts to arouse prejudices in an audience by labelling the object of the propaganda campaign as something the target audience fears, hates, loathes, or finds undesirable. This appealing to fear is commonly used; however, if not subtly crafted, it is a technique that risks backfiring.

- **Seeking Disapproval.** It is used to get the target group to withdraw their approval of an action or idea by suggesting it originated and/or is popular with the enemy.
- **Transfer.** A technique of projecting positive or negative qualities, usually blame, from one group or individual to another.
- **Vagueness.** By including generalities that, by being deliberately vague, allow for the recipients to make their own interpretations. The intention is to influence them by the use of undefined phrases, without analysing their validity or attempting to determine their reasonableness or applicability.[13,14]

PSYCHOLOGICAL WARFARE ENTERS THE DIGITAL AGE

Much resources and efforts have been invested in psychological warfare operations, but have they been successful? A question more difficult to answer than what might be assumed as measurement problems and a definition of what is considered successful must be considered. To start with, one has to distinguish between psychological operations seeking an immediate effect and longer-term ones aspiring to alter narratives. Evidence from the Second World War paints a mixed picture, and there have been comprehensive attempts to measure its success, such as that of Daniel Lerner, an OSS operative (the predecessor to the CIA) who analysed the effectiveness of various strategies. He concludes that there is little evidence that any of them were dramatically successful, except perhaps surrender instructions over loudspeakers when victory anyhow was imminent. But to objectively measure the success or failure of psychological warfare is difficult as the conditions are far from that of a controlled experiment. Also, more direct efforts such as the brainwashing of US prisoners during the Korean War only proved to be temporary; when released, the pro-communist sympathies some prisoners had displayed vanished. For longer-term propaganda campaigns, the results are even more uncertain: during the Cold War both the US and Eastern bloc spent considerable sums on psychological influence operations; however, no historians have identified psychological warfare campaigns as a root cause of the downfall of Soviet Union. Where there are ample evidence of successful propaganda operations are of the kind of incredible truths techniques have been used, whether actually true or not, that in have caused detrimental consequences, often against corporations, in the short term, and at times, over an extended period. The purpose has often been, for financial (read: stock price) or other reasons, to quickly damage their reputation by creating immediate confusion and shock in a fast and furious pace, thereby making defence arrangements and counter attacks difficult to quickly establish. This is a trend that has been exacerbated as the world has entered the digital age, where psychological warfare goes online and can be morphed into a hybrid form that has been enabled through the amalgamation that the components of digital warfare include. The digital age is proving an enabler for psychological warfare and its successful variation can be labelled as a form of blitzkrieg in the digital age. Many now convincingly argue that digital wars are constantly going on between nations, but also exposing corporates at risk as proxy targets, sometimes with nations as aggressors, sometimes sinister competitors, hacktivists, or criminal enterprises.

Chapter 3 will discuss historical incidents of war in the digital sphere, highlighting known strategies and how they evolved.

NOTES

1 Szunyogh, Béla. *Psychological Warfare; An Introduction to Ideological Propaganda and the Techniques of Psychological Warfare* (New York: William-Frederick Press, 1955) p. 13.

2 Doob, Leonard W. The Strategies of Psychological Warfare (*Public Opinion Quarterly*, Vol. 13, Issue 4 (1949)). pp. 635–644.

3 Lerner, Daniel. *Psychological Warfare against Nazi Germany: The Sykewar Campaign, D-Day to VE-Day* (Boston, MA: MIT Press, 1971).

4 Ibid.

5 Kilcullen, David. *The Accidental Guerrilla: Fighting Small Wars in the Midst of a Big One* (Oxford: Oxford University Press, Reprint Edition, 2011).

6 Ellul, Jacques. *Propaganda: The Formation of Men's Attitudes* (Translated by Konrad Kellen & Jean Lerner from original 1962 French edition *Propagandes*. New York: *Vintage Books*, 1973).

7 Qualter, Terence H. *Propaganda and Psychological Warfare* (Studies in Political Science. New York: Random House, 1962).

8 Ellul, Jacques. *Propaganda: The Formation of Men's Attitudes* (Translated by Konrad Kellen & Jean Lerner from original 1962 French edition *Propagandes*. New York: *Vintage Books*, 1973). p. 4.

9 Karlins, Marvin, & Abelson, Herbet I. *Persuasion: How Opinions and Attitudes Are Changed* (New York: Springer, 2nd edition, 1970). pp. 41–67.

10 Pratkanis, Anthony, & Aronson, Elliot. *Age of Propaganda: The Everyday Use and Abuse of Persuasion* (New York: Holt Paperbacks, 2001). pp. 167–173.

11 Jowett, Garth S., & O'Donnell, Victoria. *Propaganda & Persuasion* (Thousand Oaks, CA: SAGE Publications, Inc, 5th edition, 2011), chapter 6.

12 Headquarters; Department of the Army. *Appendix I: PSYOP Techniques* (Psychological Operations Field Manual No. 33-1, 31 August 1979).

13 Jowett, Garth S., & O'Donnell, Victoria. *Propaganda & Persuasion* (Thousand Oaks, CA: SAGE Publications, Inc; 5th edition, 2011), chapter 6.

14 Headquarters; Department of the Army. *Appendix I: PSYOP Techniques* (Psychological Operations Field Manual No. 33-1, 31 August 1979).

3

WHAT IS DIGITAL WARFARE?

…jeder Angriff muß mit einem Verteidigen endigen…
…every attack must lead to a defence…

Carl von Clausewitz (1780–1831),
legendary German war strategist

DEFINING DIGITAL WARFARE, IS IT PERHAPS MORE THAN MEETS THE EYE?

Digital warfare, also commonly known as cyber warfare or information warfare, covers three main areas:

1 **Espionage**, retrieving information about an opponent, also through illicit means such as hacking, which includes theft of intellectual property
2 **Psychological warfare**, as described in the previous chapter and which in the spirit of Clausewitz often are part of political pressure campaigns, but more and more also targets corporations
3 **Sabotage**, which includes
   • **Denying access to electronic services:** by preventing networks and computers from working properly and thereby reducing, or even eliminating, an opponent's operations and disrupting the distribution of information and services

- **Causing damage to data or physical equipment:** destroying or distorting information, or in the physical world abusing computer-controlled equipment to shut down power grids or to destroy applications and tools

Whilst digital warfare can be broken down into distinct areas as mentioned above, as of yet no consensus definition of it exists, which is noteworthy from an international law perspective, something that becomes problematic as whether or not to include these as acts of war. Semantics play a role here as warfare need not equate to formal war, and thus falls outside the legal definition of war, which triggers certain consequences. An illustrative example is Russia blocking and attempting to take down Georgia's access to internet during the conflict in 2008, something which might not, then at least, violate international accords. But if a private company, whether assisting a government or not, shuts down another nation's internet access, that would constitute a clear violation. It also exemplifies that to craft a definition is further complicated by whom are considered as combatants, if they are state actors or private enterprises, or even individuals. A reverse consideration might also apply, as a military force releasing a virus to cause damage to an opponent's infrastructure during a declared war would of course constitute an act of war but a single hacker doing the same in that conflict might not be considered as an act of war. Given these ambiguities, a case is being made for a "Digital Geneva Convention," but so far the major nations appear uninterested, possibly as they want to reserve the right to use and fully understand the potential of digital warfare tools before agreeing to more formalised agreements. There are, however, some definitions to ringfence war activities in the digital sphere, for example the European Union's definition of cyber warfare, which makes a point that it needs to target another state, reads (Figure 3.1):

> Cyber warfare refers to any action by a state, group or criminal organisation facilitated by or using cyberspace targeting another state.[1]

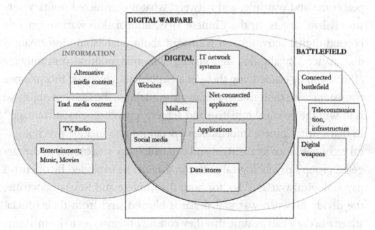

Figure 3.1 A graphical overview highlighting the distinctions between information, the digital sphere and battlefields.

For the purpose of this book, we define digital warfare as follows:

> Digital warfare is a concerted effort with a clear goal to impose one's will through subjugation by force or threat of force on another nation, organisation or corporation utilising digital tools.

There is, however, a noted difference in how authoritarian regimes, such as China and Russia, view warfare vis-à-vis the traditional western view. It is probably best described by a quote from a much-referenced article by General Valery Gerasimov, Chief of the Russian General Staff:

> The information space opens wide asymmetrical possibilities for reducing the fighting potential of the enemy. In north Africa, we witnessed the use of technologies for influencing state structures and the population with the help of information networks. It is necessary to perfect activities in the information space, including the defense of our own objects.[2]

The Chinese People's Liberation Army's (PLA) view is also broader than the traditional Western one, making no clear distinction between peacetime and wartime, and between what is considered military versus civilian targets. In the Chinese view, information warfare extends beyond digital activities and is instead about establishing information dominance.[3] By aligning diplomatic, economic, political, and military efforts, and by embedding these in an information context in a manner consistent with their military strategic guidelines, the Chinese objective is to win the political initiative and achieve a psychological advantage.[4] In that spirit, Chinese information operations also include psychological reconnaissance to ascertain and determine any weaknesses in the targeted group's psychological outlooks that can be exploited by offensive psychological warfare.[5] So, for both the Chinese and Russian doctrine, the divide between war and peace is blurred, and from their official statements one can assume that they consider themselves to be in a constant state of (information) war. In particular for the Chinese regime to control information and monopolise what is considered as unquestionable truths, to which no deviation from its citizens are accepted, are seen as a pivotal instrument to secure their political power. This as China considers the state as ultimately having control over its citizens and private corporations, enforcing that they are legally obliged to collect information deemed necessary for state security. In effect, it means that the division between civilian and soldiers has been invalidated, as they, on request, are forced to act as spies or digital soldiers. Digital warfare is being regarded as a cheaper, less risky strategy to reach softer political objectives and in many instances covertly attack opponents. In this perspective the advancement of new technologies and tools have allowed for the digital sphere to become a testing ground to initiate escalating degrees of warfare, many times operating under anonymity. It is proving to be an area of continuous trial-and-error.

CHARACTERISTICS OF DIGITAL WARFARE

Digital warfare has several characteristics that differentiates it from traditional warfare, both conceptually and practically. These unique characteristics structured through an acronym, CHAOS, are as follows:

- **Cheap**. Digital warfare is a very cost-efficient undertaking versus the damage it can create, closing down large parts of a country's infrastructure and in effect holding it hostage. Unlike military deployment, the levels of permanent destruction and collateral damage are typically small with low mortality rates, although doomsday scenarios using solely a digital arsenal can be fathomed and envisioned. The objective with digital warfare takes more of a black mail approach, threatening to force a society or corporation into submission by either communicating or effecting the capacity to shut down or sabotage vital functions rather than a physical occupation of territories or destruction to reach desired objectives.

- **Hit-and-run**. Digital attacks rely on exploiting weaknesses in an opponent's networks and systems. Once an attack has been executed and the weakness revealed, the defender can seek to remedy it, basically making further attacks depending on that specific technology rendered more or less useless. As the global security community is coordinating efforts to fix discovered loopholes, digital defense applications can be distributed relatively quickly. This makes the window of opportunity to exploit security gaps for the digital warrior being often of a one-off hit-and-run opportunity.

- **Anonymity**. Historically in war, combatants were always known, because traditionally an attack was preceded by a declaration of war. In digital warfare, the identity of the attacker is no longer always known. A digital weapon can just be a piece of code written by anyone with reasonable programming skills and an unsavoury character, and what and whom he represents might never be fully ascertained.

- **Opportunistic**. Newly launched technologies provide possibilities for the digital warrior to find weaknesses that might provide the launch of an assault, and with a constant flow of upgrades, the scope for attacks will be ample for the tech-savvy combatant. There might also be certain events that lend themselves to attacks, which could be political campaigns, economic or financial circumstances, or societal issues that could be exacerbated through the deployment of digital warfare tools.

- **Scalability**. Digital weapons are both easy and strategically capable of being amalgamated in a hybrid warfare strategy. It allows for a scalable approach to war, where the digital part of it can fall in a sort of twilight zone between peace and war and provide a unique ability to scale an attack as required. Launching a virus or initiating a psychological warfare operation is not as definite as firing the first bullet or dropping the first bomb in a conflict. It can also much more selectively and in a proxy manner choose its opponents, such as that of an organisation, a corporation or even an individual affiliated with its main opponent and from there escalate to wide-ranging digital warfare attacks that paralyses society at large.

It is in this context also important to distinguish between targeted and indiscriminate attacks. Targeted attacks focus on specific individuals or organisations, seeking to obtain intelligence or engage in some kind of destructive activities, whereas an indiscriminate attack might seek to effectively shut down or block the entire internet access of a country.

A TAXONOMY OF DIGITAL ATTACKS

Digital attacks come in many forms, depending on access to malware but also type of target. Broadly, an attack can be active or passive. An "active attack" attempts to sabotage systems or affect their operations whereas a "passive attack" seeks to gather and make use of information from the systems but does not seek to damage them as that would compromise the covert mission. One also needs to categorise the perpetrator, as an attack can be orchestrated by an insider or from outside the organisation. An inside attack is initiated by an individual or group, typically an employee, already with some authorisation to access system resources, who decided to use this privilege maliciously. An outside attack is administrated by someone not privy to the access perimeter, seeking to get inside the system through illicit entrance by having identified security vulnerabilities that can be exploited. These outside attackers could range from hostile governments to criminal groups, and even disgruntled individuals. The attacks can also be classified according to their origin, such as whether it is conducted using one or more computers, the latter being referred to as a distributed attack. Attacks can be distinguished on the vulnerabilities they are targeting, such as concentrated on network mechanisms or host features. The variety of attack types can be outlined as follows.

PASSIVE TYPES OF ATTACKS

- Computer and network surveillance
- Network
  - **Wiretapping**. Wiretapping is achieved either through the placement of a monitoring device informally known as a bug on the wire in question or through built-in mechanisms in other communication technologies. Packet sniffers – programs used to capture data being transmitted on a network – are a commonly used modern-day wiretapping tool. A variety of other tools, such as wiretap Trojans, are used for different applications.
  - **Fibre tapping**. Fibre tapping uses a network tap method that extracts signal from an optical fibre without breaking the connection. Tapping of optical fibre allows diverting some of the signal being transmitted in the core of the fibre into another fibre or a detector.
  - **Port scan**. A port scan is an attack that sends client requests to a range of server port addresses on a host, with the goal of finding an active port and exploiting a known vulnerability of that service. It is often the first step of reconnaissance used by hackers when trying to infiltrate a network or steal/destroy sensitive data.
  - **Idle scan**. The idle scan is a TCP port scan method that consists of sending spoofed packets to a computer to find out what services are available. This is accomplished by impersonating

another computer whose network traffic is very slow or non-existent. This could be an idle computer, referred to as a zombie.

- Host
  - **Keystroke logging**. It is the action of recording (logging) the keys struck on a keyboard, typically covertly, so that the person using the keyboard is unaware that their actions are being monitored. Data can then be retrieved by the person operating the logging program.
  - **Data scraping**. A technique in which a program covertly extracts data from human-readable output coming from another program.
  - **Backdoor**. A backdoor is a piece of code deliberately coded into a piece of software that allows someone to have access to the system on which it is loaded. Usually it is undesirable for backdoors to be inserted because they can be exploited by hackers to gain access.

ACTIVE TYPES OF ATTACKS

- Denial-of-service (DoS) attack
  - Distributed denial-of-service (DDoS) attack
- **Spoofing**. A spoofing attack is a situation in which a person or program successfully identifies as another by falsifying data seeking to gain an illegitimate advantage.
- **Mixed threat attack**. Mixed threat attacks generally try to exploit multiple vulnerabilities to get into a system. By launching multiple diverse attacks in parallel, the attacker can exploit more entry points than with just a single attack. Because these threats are based on multiple single attacks, they are much harder to detect.
- Network
  - **Man-in-the-middle**. It is an attack where the attacker secretly relays and possibly alters the communications between two parties who believe that they are directly communicating with each other. The attacker must be able to intercept all relevant

messages passing between the two victims and inject new ones. For example, an attacker within the reception range of an unencrypted Wi-Fi access point could insert themselves as a man-in-the-middle.

- **Man-in-the-browser**. It is a variation of the man-in-the-middle attack where an attacker is able to insert himself into the communications channel between two trusting parties by compromising a web browser used by one of the parties for the purpose of eavesdropping, data theft, and/or session tampering.

- **ARP (Address Resolution Protocol) poisoning**. ARP spoofing is a type of attack in which a malicious actor sends falsified ARP messages over a local area network. This results in the linking of an attacker's media access control address with the IP address of a legitimate computer or server on the network. Once the attacker's media access control address is connected to an authentic IP address, the attacker will begin receiving any data that is intended for that IP address. ARP spoofing can enable malicious parties to intercept, modify or even stop data in transit.

- **Ping flood**. A ping flood is a simple DoS attack where the attacker overwhelms the victim with ICMP (internet control message protocol) "echo request" (ping) packets. This is most effective by using the flood option of ping which sends ICMP packets as fast as possible without waiting for replies.

- **Ping of death**. A ping of death is a type of attack on a computer system that involves sending a malformed or otherwise malicious ping to a computer. It is a type of denial-of-service attack in which an attacker attempts to crash, destabilise, or freeze the targeted computer or service by sending malformed or oversized packets using a simple ping command.

- **Smurf attack**. A Smurf attack is a form of a DDoS attack that renders computer networks inoperable. The Smurf program accomplishes this by exploiting vulnerabilities of the Internet Protocol and ICMP.

- Host
  - **Stack overflow**. A staple among hackers, also known as stack smashing. If the affected program is running with special privileges, or accepts data from untrusted network hosts, such as a webserver, then the bug is a potential security vulnerability. If the stack buffer is filled with data supplied from an untrusted user, then that user can corrupt the stack in such a way as to inject executable code into the running program and take control of the process.
  - **Buffer overflow**. Attackers exploit buffer overflow issues by overwriting the memory of an application. This changes the execution path of the program, triggering a response that damages files or exposes private information. For example, an attacker may introduce extra code, sending new instructions to the application to gain access to IT systems. If attackers know the memory layout of a program, they can intentionally feed input that the buffer cannot store, and overwrite areas that hold executable code, replacing it with their own code.
  - **Heap overflow**. It is a type of buffer overflow that occurs in the heap data area. Heap overflows are exploitable in a different manner to that of stack overflows. Memory on the heap is dynamically allocated at runtime and typically contains program data. Exploitation is performed by corrupting this data in specific ways to cause the application to overwrite internal structures such as linked list pointers.
  - **Format string attack**. A format string attack occurs when the submitted data of an input string is evaluated as a command by the application. In this way, the attacker could execute code, read the stack, or cause a segmentation fault in the running application, causing new behaviours that could compromise the security or the stability of the system.
- Syntactic attacks
  - **Virus**. A virus is a self-replicating program that can attach itself to other programs or files in order to reproduce and multiply itself. To avoid detection, the virus often hides in

unlikely locations in the memory of a computer system and attaches itself to whatever file it sees fit to execute its code. It can also change its digital footprint each time it replicates, making it harder to track down in the computer. A virus is a type of malicious code or program written to alter the way computer operates and is designed to spread from one computer to another. A virus operates by inserting or attaching itself to a legitimate program or document that supports macros in order to execute its code. In the process, a virus has the potential to cause unexpected or damaging effects, such as harming the system software by corrupting or destroying data.

- **Worms**. A worm, unlike a virus, does not need another file or program to copy itself as it is a self-sustaining running program. Worms replicate over networks by using protocols. Worms can modify and delete files, and they can even inject additional malicious software onto a computer. Sometimes a computer worm's purpose is only to make copies of itself over and over, depleting system resources, such as hard drive space or bandwidth, by overloading a shared network. In addition to wreaking havoc on a computer's resources, worms can also steal data, install a backdoor, and allow a hacker to gain control over a computer and its system settings.
- **Trojan horse**. A Trojan horse is designed to perform legitimate tasks but it also performs unknown and unwanted activity. It can be the basis of many viruses and worms installing onto the computer as keyboard loggers and backdoor software. Trojans can be imbedded in trial versions of software and can gather additional intelligence about the target without the person even knowing it happening.
- Semantic attacks
  - A semantic attack is the modification and dissemination of correct and incorrect information. Information modified could have been done without the use of computers even though new opportunities can be found by using them.

THE COMPONENTS OF A DEFENCE FRAMEWORK

To adequately manage and mitigate such a disparate plethora of attacks executed through varying means and with differing motives, an information security standard has been established to generically determine the level of security labelled the *CIA triad*, and no, it has nothing to do with the US intelligence agency bearing the same acronym. Instead it refers to three key factors: *confidentiality, integrity,* and *availability* of resources and the risk of these being compromised.

Confidentiality means controlling the access to proprietary data in order to prevent unauthorised disclosure. Countermeasures to protect confidentiality include:

- data and labelling through establishing access controls and authentication mechanisms
- encryption of data in process, in transit, and in storage
- *steganography*, remote wipe capabilities, and adequate education and training for all individuals with access to data

Integrity is about ensuring that data has not been fraudulently manipulated and therefore compromising it. The data need to, at all times, be correct, authentic, and reliable. Ensuring integrity involves protecting data in use, in transit (such as when sending an email or uploading or downloading a file), and when it is stored. Countermeasures that protect data integrity include encryption, hashing, digital signatures, digital certificates, intrusion detection systems, auditing, version control, and strong authentication mechanisms and access controls. The concept of integrity is broader than merely covering data. It is also related to *non-repudiation*, meaning the inability to deny something, such as by using digital signatures in email; for example a sender cannot deny having sent a message, and the recipient cannot claim the message received was different from the one sent.

Finally, availability, systems, applications, and data are of little value to a corporation and its users if they are not accessible as and when needed. Thus, availability means that networks, systems, and applications are up and running to ensure that authorised users have timely, reliable access to resources as and when they are needed. Denial-of-service attack, in which the performance of a system, website, web-based application, or web-based service is intentionally and maliciously degraded, or the system becomes completely unreachable, is a favoured tactic amongst hackers to disrupt availability. But there are of course features beyond undesignated attacks that can interrupt availability, including hardware or software failure, power failure, natural disasters, and human errors. Countermeasures to help ensure availability include redundancy in servers, networks, applications, and services; hardware fault tolerance for servers and storage; regular software patching and system upgrades; backups; comprehensive disaster recovery plans; and DoS protection solutions. Potentially, there is also a risk of collateral damage, spilling over to further parts of the organisation, and not unusually also affecting third parties, such as customers and suppliers.

The three factors of the CIA triad form the edifice of a corporation's security infrastructure, as by upholding them the risk of digital attacks is being reduced. Thus, digital security arrangements can be evaluated by gauging known threats and vulnerabilities based on the potential impact they might have on confidentiality, integrity, and availability of a corporation's data, applications, and critical systems.

To illustrate the various aspects of digital warfare, ranked in the order of complexity and effort, the remainder of this chapter will highlight some case studies that describe strategic considerations and the particular digital weapons that were deployed.

Case Study Sabotage

Anyone who logged into to the US Navy's website in April 1999, in the midst of their engagement in the civil war in former Yugoslavia, was highly surprised to find profanities and insults rather than the expected information. There were also a few NATO web servers that did not respond at all and websites that had been overwritten with anti-US propaganda or slogans.[6] On 27 April 2007, the citizens of Estonia woke up noticing that their internet had started to slow down and that government and domestic news websites were no longer accessible. The malfunctioning internet connection remained throughout May to the point where all internet services had slowed down significantly, especially email services. It was difficult to access websites outside Estonia and online banking services were at times down for hours, causing disruption and harm to a society that had become highly reliant on online connectivity.[7] A similar incident occurred in Georgia on 8 August 2008, but being a far less connected society, the detrimental effects were less and it managed to keep vital services intact. And in both Israel and South Korea there were defacement attacks on governmental websites during 2009. What had happened in all these cases? The digital attack against the US in 1999 coincided with the ongoing war in former Yugoslavia, the Estonian attack occurred during a controversy with Russia, and Georgia was engaged in war. The Israeli defacements attacks were most likely part of the conflict they were engaged in with the Hamas terrorist group, and the South Korean and North Korean relationship in 2009 was particularly strenuous. These attacks are technically relatively unsophisticated and can be launched without too much preparatory work. Website defacement is basically about getting access to websites or systems, usually not part of a core computer network, that are interfacing the internet, by cracking the passwords of the users granted access to edit content. Website defacement is a relatively minor transgression as it mostly amounts to vandalism, with the restoring of the original content being a fairly straightforward task, embarrassing yes, but often fixed within a few hours. Blocking websites is known as denial of service (DoS) and is simply the overloading of internet facing servers by sending large amounts of requests, a technique that has been commonplace over the last two decades. A large number of computers can be compromised or hijacked and combined into a *botnet* that can be used to send huge amounts of requests in what is known as a DDoS attack.[8,9] One of the largest botnets found to date, referred to as 3*ve*, consisted of 1.7 million computers operating in concert.[10] These types of attacks can effectively, however typically only for a relatively limited period of time (in the case of Estonia being unusually long), shut down vital service providers from transmitting and receiving information.

Case Study Espionage

Since the earliest days of computers, hackers have had something of the folklore's underground hero status, and much has been written about the excitement and thrill of hacking some government's or big corporation's computer systems just for the sake of it, proving one's technical skills and cognitive prowess. In most cases, there was no sinister intent seeking to commercially exploit the illicitly gained information, but it was rather an act of showing off in the underground communities that the hackers were affiliated to. However, before long, intelligence agencies started to employ their own hackers to retrieve information, distinctly easier and less risky ventures than having to recruit spies that physically had to steal or copy documents at location.

The first known notable case of digital espionage occurred in 1998 and has become known as the *Moonlight Maze* incident. The US military had noticed what appeared to be an advanced, likely government-sponsored, attack on the Pentagon and other governmental agencies, such as NASA and the Department of Energy, where large numbers of non-classified, yet sensitive, documents had been downloaded and stolen.[11] The investigators traced the origin of the attack to a computer outside Moscow, but no formal legal procedures were ever made, and the details of the case are still classified. It was eventually discovered that the hackers had been able to access the systems for 2 years, using for the time advanced hacking tactics to create backdoors which allowed them entrance to the systems.

In 2003, the US once again identified what appeared to be coordinated state-sponsored attacks, this time against defence contractors such as Lockheed-Martin and Sandia, but also against secure networks involving military bases and installations. This attack was designated to a group that was referred to as an "advanced persistent threat" named *Titan Rain*. Advanced persistent threat has in the nomenclature of digital security come to mean an advanced hacker group with the capacity for extended attacks against multiple targets simultaneously; however, their *modus operandi* usually leaves behavioural patterns that provide evidence for law enforcement. The hacker group Titan Rain continued to launch attacks on several other countries and defence contractors, including the United Kingdom and BAE in 2008.

In 2010, Google noticed an intrusion, that has come to be known as "Operation Aurora" originating in 2009. Google had been targeted through a technique labelled "spearphishing," which means targeting specific email recipients with an infected mail including a bug conjuring the recipient to click on a link in the email which allows for the attacker to get hold of their password or getting access to their computers. Google noticed that for the perpetrators a primary goal was seeking to get access to Chinese dissident's email accounts, and suspecting the Chinese authorities behind it led to Google withdrawing cooperation projects with the Chinese government in 2010.[12,13]

By targeting specific users with bespoke contents rather than generic distribution, the risk of detection is generally smaller, and administrators and antivirus software often might oversee blocking these emails. Spearphishing is considered to have a higher success rate in deceiving its recipients as opposed to phishing, where huge amounts of standardised emails are distributed to a designated group in a shotgun approach, seeking to deceive as many as possible, and then sifting through information in the quest for account statements, personal details, or similar data considered to hold value. More recently, a hacker group got access to code libraries in GitHub, a hosting service for software development and version control, where they were not only able to steal software code, but their illicit access provided them with the possibility to modify code and covertly create security gaps in third-party software that can be exploited, putting millions of users at risk for future attacks.

Whilst digital espionage should be distinguished from digital warfare, it is, however, often part of a preparatory phase prior to commencing with digital warfare activities. Its true extent can at best only be guesstimated, as efforts to collect comprehensive statistics on security breaches are marred with extensive measurement problems, given the reputational risk of being exposed with having substandard IT security arrangements carry. But that digital intrusions with the intent of illegally accessing information are commonplace and accelerating, both in absolute and relative numbers, is generally agreed upon, increasingly targeting corporations.

Case Study Destruction

When the employees of the Saudi Arabian firm Aramco walked into their office on 15th August 2012, they quickly noticed that their computers were unusable; and attack affected almost all of their 30,000 computers. They were not able to access data, and it took over a week before they were operating normally again. A disgruntled employee was blamed for the incident; however, an investigation later pointed fingers at the Iranian government which the employee was accused to clandestinely work for, coordinated by a group called "Cutting Sword of Justice" that came to take responsibility for the incident. Destroying data is more difficult than just getting read-write access to a computer system, as the writing and preparation of files usually follows a controlled sequence, meaning that to permanently destroy data, an administrator-level access is required, as typically a file deleted is in effect just hidden on the hard drive and can easily be recovered and retrieved. Destructive viruses of this nature have been around since the mid-1980s, an early example is the "Jerusalem computer virus" capable of destroying all executable files in computers it had infected, but only on Fridays the 13th, a legendary prank that still was able to cause considerable damage. An approach preferred by criminal groups is to only encrypt data, not permanently delete it, and then demand money for a decryption key, a concept known as *ransomware*; its first known case dates back to 1989.[14]

That countries, as part of digital warfare operations, are involved in actual destruction of data or software is relatively rare; however, one of the most famous cases was a state-sponsored one and it has come to be known as one of the most famous and spectacular attacks, *Stuxnet*. It was designed to destroy software enabling the centrifuges that Iran used for its nuclear enrichment program. When it was discovered in 2010, and deconstructed and reviewed by independent security analysts, its highly advanced capabilities caused shockwaves amongst IT security specialists. Stuxnet was able to destroy physical hardware, a feature that few at the time thought possible, and whilst there had been some viruses able to destruct a disk drive inside a computer, something of the scale of Stuxnet was not seen as feasible. It was able to do so by attacking the industrial control systems and through these reach the Iranian network computers' programmable logic controllers (PLC) from where the timers and switches of the actual centrifuges were administered and operated. These types of systems required intrinsic knowledge of their design to craft targeted programs seeking their destruction. The Stuxnet virus was able to cause the centrifuge to speed up, slow down, and return to normal operating speed over and over, which eventually wore out the centrifuges and triggered a malfunctioning but it was something the system operators did not detect as they outwardly appeared to be running normally. It was reported that the virus in effect destroyed 1,000 out of the 5,000 centrifuges used as part of the nuclear enrichment program. The type of industrial computer systems that the Iranians were using were air-gapped, meaning that they were not connected to the internet at all, this as a standard security precaution, making external digital attacks against them exceptionally difficult to conduct. The Stuxnet attackers, however, relied on social engineering to exploit security flaws in the behaviour of the operators in charge, this by realising that they were likely using memory sticks to move data between computers, including some with an internet connection, making it a viable insertion point for infecting the ringfenced computers. This is normally a safe procedure considering that without a transmission effect but due to a flaw in Microsoft Windows, a so-called *zero-day-vulnerability*, the virus could be transmitted and infect the industrial computer systems controlling the centrifuges. The hacker also identified other weaknesses in Windows that were utilised to plant the virus. Eventually, it was confirmed that it was the US and Israeli intelligence services that were behind Stuxnet through a group that became known as the "Equation Group." The news that government agencies were behind the attack drew a lot of criticism against them, as they had not informed Microsoft of the flaws they had identified, essentially leaving any user of Windows at risk and possibly also being exploited in other unreported cases.[15]

RATIONALE FOR DIGITAL WARFARE

Through the description of the above case studies, the contrasts between digital warfare and conventional warfare can be distinguished and highlighted. Digital warfare is by and large a non-lethal war, lives are generally not at risk, albeit the indirect collateral damages that can occur by shutting down vital systems. It is drastically cheaper than boots on ground with no risk of personnel. It is to some extent possible to be conducted hiding under anonymity, making it very hard to attribute responsibility for an attack. Obfuscation is an important concept in particular hacker attacks, going so far as hacker groups trying to copy signature code other hacker groups are (in)famous for. However, the originators of larger-scale attacks, especially against countries, tend to be revealed given the complexity and advanced skill they usually require, something only a few independent hacker groups can muster, hence the list of potential suspects tend to be quite few, with almost all of them having at least some state affiliation, albeit loose. From a legal perspective, many of these digital warfare techniques are not regulated under any international legislation and would therefore not be classified as acts of war, but with the exception of psychological warfare campaigns, most would however be considered as crimes.

THE EXECUTION OF A DIGITAL WARFARE ATTACK

A number of tools need to be deployed in attacking or hacking a system as part of a digital warfare operation and it typically is arranged through a sequential series of steps. There are several frameworks that distinguish these; however most follow certain generic procedures that will be described below, highlighted through the Lockheed Martin "cyber kill chain" (Figure 3.2). For each step, there is a variety of tools and techniques that can be used by the attacker, and subsequently for each step the defender has possibilities to establish preventive measures. These would cover the espionage, sabotage, and destruction categories of digital warfare; the psychological operations follow a separate model, which was described in Chapter 2 but can be coordinated for heightened impact.

Once the goals and the objectives with a digital attack have been formulated and set, it typically follows the seven ensuing steps:

1 **Reconnaissance**. Collection and analysis of data on target(s), seeking to identify vulnerabilities that can be exploited.

2 **Weaponise**. Create or utilise tools that can access and intrude the identified vulnerabilities.

3 **Intrusion**. Activate the weaponised malware to attack the targeted computer networks or systems.

4 **Exploit and installation**. Plant the malware inside the targeted networks or systems. Collect data or identify data of interest. Establish persistence and obfuscation, such as by upgrading the code to remain covert and cover the tracks of the illicit activities.

5 **Command and control**. Take control of the systems, ideally by installing remote control access and/or have tools to capture commands from command nodes;

6 **Act**. Upload the collected data or execute commands to damage or encrypt systems.

7 **Disguise**. A final step that is arguably often added. This step is the hiding and deleting of the traces of the digital attack, and the techniques used are usually the same as in the Exploit and Installation step.

Figure 3.2 Strategic steps when planning and executing a digital warfare attack.

For the simplest forms of attacks such as DoS, only steps 2 and 4 are relevant, webpage defacements would follow steps 2–4. The following sections will detail each step, adding features through describing the 2017 "NotPetya" attack in Ukraine, which probably is one of the incidents coming closest to a full-scale digital warfare.[16] NotPetya was what seemed to be a ransomware virus that started to spread in June 2017 and was initially attributed to some profit-seeking criminal hacker group. It eventually emerged that it instead was a disguised digital attack targeting Ukraine with Russia attributed as perpetrator, and CIA found it likely that the Russian military intelligence service, GRU, had orchestrated the attack, although this has been vehemently denied by Russia.[17] Motivation for Russia was however not lacking, as it was in conflict with Ukraine at the time.

The NotPetya virus erased data from computers of state-owned banks, energy firms, and government agencies and departments, spreading to also private corporations, eventually causing major harm outside Ukraine as well. The cost of the attack is estimated to be around 10 billion USD, including the costs of trying to retrieve and restore lost data. It affected much of Ukraine's infrastructure, an airport was locked down and even the monitoring systems of the Chernobyl nuclear plant were damaged.[18]

The actual goal of the attack has still not been ascertained; however, it appears that it was a power demonstration aimed at showing the might of Russia, being able to do significant harm on a broad front against Ukraine's infrastructure. However, the attackers did show restrains as with the access they had gained over infrastructure systems they had the possibility to create physical damage but avoided doing so, accentuating the impression of a demonstration of power.

RECONNAISSANCE

Reconnaissance means conducting research on the target with a view to identify opportunities and weaknesses in the opponent's security arrangements. It includes both a technical perspective, such as gaining information on what systems they are using, and a human perspective, who are the employees with access to the systems and ascertaining whether they can be compromised in later steps.

Examples
- By using network scanners to identify the targeted computers that interface with the web, one can determine the behaviour of the outgoing internet traffic and study logs from connected systems.
- Employing traditional espionage and information gathering techniques, such as collating and analysing media coverage on what networks and systems the targets are using could include attending conferences to connect and conjure employees suspected of holding possession of sensitive information. This also includes collecting personal profiles from various social media networks.
- One can gather personal data from other hacker attacks, including financial status or information that can be exploited for blackmail and coercion.

The NotPetya Case
In the NotPetya case, it seems likely that the attacker had made a very in-depth reconnaissance and had been able to identify significant vulnerabilities, both from a human intelligence perspective and an analysis of computers and networks. As part of the reconnaissance phase, the attacker had identified that a domestic accounting software known as MeDoc had 400,000 customers and represented about 90% of the local firms in Ukraine, making it an efficient vehicle to launch malware from and initiate the attack. Surveillance applications probably had been used for a long time to monitor activity before the attack was launched. Not only was the MeDoc software used for accounting purposes but it also

included links to corporate tax registration details, providing a path to identify specific targets at a very detailed level.[19,20]

WEAPONISE

After recognising a suitable technical target for an attack, malware must be planted. Typically these are not bespokenly developed; rather, the attackers use prepared toolkits which are deployed seeking to exploit what is found to be vulnerabilities in the target systems. The malware, coupled with the exploitable vulnerability, are weaponised into a *payload*, such as when infiltrating through files with decoy documents being presented to the victims through email for instance. Installed backdoors and the appropriate command and control infrastructure are selected for the operation. Finally, the backdoors are compiled and the payload weaponised.

Examples
A lot of tools are open source which can be downloaded and modified by anyone. These are often combined into malware toolkits. However, as these are publicly available, antivirus software are continuously upgraded to recognise and block them, hence their lifespan as a potent virus is relatively short and limited. Malware customised for designated attacks are therefore more likely to circumvent standardised antivirus software, by adjusting open source tools to make them harder to detect.

The NotPetya Case
The NotPetya virus was an adapted version of an older ransomware known as "Petya," hence the name NotPetya, where the code had been enhanced to cause more damage by encrypting all infected files and wiping out some of them, making the recovery of data more complicated.

INTRUSION

Intrusion is the act of getting the malware planted, preferably inside firewalls and other security measures, to commence the operations on the targets computer systems. It could be to further distribute malware inside the network and/or launch its destructive activities.

Examples
- The intrusion can be an adversary controlled delivery, which is typically directed against web servers.
- The intrusion can be an adversary released delivery through malicious email, malware on memory sticks, social media interactions, or so-called watering holes, compromised websites where a person unknowingly installs an application with the malicious code.

The NotPetya Case

The attacker was able to get into the MeDoc mechanism that was used to distribute and install updates to clients. It was a variation of compromising the application itself and distribute the malicious code having it installed unwittingly at the end users' computers. Initially, the attack was attributed to a large-scale phishing operation, as the virus appeared to spread so randomly and efficiently, but eventually an investigation concluded that the MeDoc application and distribution system was the source, leading Ukrainian law enforcement to raid the software maker's office. Obviously, an attack of this enormous scale did not go unnoticed and caught the attention of the global security software community, and hence became a one-off case as the security gaps that allowed the virus to transmit and spread were closed down to prevent future attacks. This highlights the strategic perspective a digital warrior must consider before launching an attack of such a public nature, the *modus operandi* will be carefully studied by law enforcement and software security experts making sure that any identified security gaps are plugged, not to be exploited again. This forces an attacker to always make sure that he is ahead of the technological curve, realising that a knowledge advantage once used, only occasionally can be recycled.

EXPLOIT AND INSTALLATION

The phrase *zero day* is often used to refer to the exploit code applied, through an identified vulnerability, to gain access to the system. This can be done through software, hardware, or any security weaknesses identified in human behaviour, as described in the previous step. Once the attacker is able to execute code inside the system, the goal typically becomes to try to get higher administrative privileges that provide access to more data and computers. As part of this step, the attacker seeks to install backdoors and/or web shells on web servers to secure their foothold and points of persistence by adding capabilities such as AutoRun keys. It is also important to try to hide the presence of malware by removing traces of the actions and use of exploit entrance points, to avoid detection through security scans that monitor the networks and review usage patterns. A secure network would notice if the typical standard user is trying to request, or even list, sensitive data, and a user would, eventually at least, notice if their device is using up an excessive amount of resources as memory, disk space or network capacity. It becomes something of a hide-and-seek game between the intruder and security software and its analysts, as the intruder constantly needs to make sure they stay ahead of updates of security software that risk exposing active malware.

Examples
- installing a backdoor capable of implanting additional and potentially more damaging malware in addition to the software that established the first foothold inside the system
- the use of polymorphic techniques, which means writing code that can change its characteristics to avoid detection, polymorphism, or even completely rewrite its own code, metamorphism
- by trying to get hold of other users' passwords and thereby use several accounts to hide in the systems, the opportunity to hide is facilitated and likely improves the chance of getting access to higher security levels
- the creation of data sniffers able to identify and pinpoint "interesting" data

- hiding stolen data by emulating it as other data on the memory disk or encrypting it so it will not be noticed
- removing traces of the intrusion and the covertly planted malware, including deleting logs and over time removing older versions that might be detected by updated security software
- mapping the network and systems, as this will help write new targeted malware that can break into other computers and systems, or independently exist
- Using the foothold to collect information to gain insights on other users will help to write new targeted spear-phishing mail attacks against more users higher up in the security hierarchy. A system administrator is more likely to click on a link or install a piece of software if it seems to come from a fellow colleague rather than from an outsider.

The NotPetya Case

The name NotPetya comes from the fact that the weaponisers in this attack added a lot of new functionality to the older Petya malware, and it quickly became obvious it was not Petya. One of the newly added functionality was a "worm," a piece of code that is able to spread itself across the system. Another new feature was Mimikatz, a tool that could steal passwords of other users from the memory of computers with a Windows operating system where multiple users had logged in. The new functionalities allowed the NotPetya to rapidly spread far beyond the users of the MeDoc accounting software. In fact, security researchers were surprised that the attack was so far reaching in such a short time that they assumed it was a more indiscriminately generic attack.

Even though the target was Ukrainian organisations, the virus spread outside its borders, ending up causing huge costs also to multinational companies and wreaking havoc on parts of global supply chains. For instance, the Danish logistics giant Maersk was among those being infected by the NotPetya virus. It also caused their systems to shut down, making it impossible to handle shipments, bringing their logistics activities to a halt for several days. Through their global presence, they were eventually able to restore service by having and using computers geographically distant and somewhat isolated, such as in Africa, that were unaffected by the virus. It was estimated that the incident ended up costing Maersk more than 200 million USD.

COMMAND AND CONTROL

After the malware has established and spread inside the target systems, it is important to maintain control over it. It means setting up a control and command structure that is able to communicate with the planted malware. Ideally, this would include installing backdoors that allows taking remote control of systems. The most common command and control channels are the web, the Domain Name System, and email protocols.

Examples
- Installing remote control software either with command line commands or even commercial packages that lets you control the computer's mouse and screen: This happened in the attack on Ukraine's power grid that used the commercial *PCAnywhere* tool, and the power station operators could only helplessly watch how hackers had seized control of their computers.
- By having the code communicate with control centres, a hacker can request commands or send status updates using seemingly innocent web requests. Such an application can, for instance, contact a website to see if it should act or get commands to send the data it has received.
- Other communication forms can be utilised; for example one attack used the social media network *Telegram* to send and receive instructions. To the security staff monitoring systems, this would seem like a user chatting on his network as the data itself would be encrypted.

- This step importantly also includes how to arrange the setup for extracting the retrieved data. Common methods include either sending it through email, ftp, uploading it to a webserver, transferring it in some encrypted way, or utilising transmission control protocol.

The NotPetya Case

The attack's command and control servers were able to create backdoors into the computers it had infected. It could hide by acting as an antivirus program, and also categorised the infected accounts based on installed antivirus software. To communicate with the control servers, they used domain servers with names similar to the antivirus company ESET to try to make the communication appear legitimate. The command and control server itself was available on an open access server that included Russian-language documents explaining how to use the masked malware which helped to attribute the attack.[21]

ACT

Finally, the malware starts to act in accordance to its set objectives. This can cover a broad range of possibilities from espionage via data destruction to physical destruction. The limitations obviously hinge on the coding capabilities of the attackers but also in accordance to Clausewitz theories, namely, how severe (political) consequences that the perpetrators are able to muster.

Examples

The most common objectives are in falling order of capacity to do damage:

- cause destruction by wiping out data, prevent applications from operating, or even physically destroy vital infrastructure
- encrypting data in a criminal blackmail purpose through ransomware
- espionage, the extraction of commercially, politically, or in other ways valuable information

The NotPetya Case

The objective of the NotPetya attack was initially considered to be a blackmail operation, this by encrypting entire memory drives and displaying a message to the affected users requesting a ransom in order to release the data again. However, further analysis proved this to be a false objective, as the provided decryption keys were not functioning, meaning that even if someone had paid the ransom, it would not be possible to decrypt the affected memories, rendering the data in effect permanently destroyed. The investigation also found that some infected disks had actually been destroyed by the virus.

NOTES

1   The European Union Agency for Cybersecurity (ENISA). *ENISA Overview of Cyber-security and Related Terminology* (September 2017). https://www.enisa.europa.eu/publications/enisa-position-papers-and-opinions/enisa-overview-of-cybersecurity-and-related-terminology (accessed 1 January 2021).

2   Valery, Gerasimov. *The Value of Science in Prediction* (Military-Industrial Kurier, 27 February 2013). https://vpk-news.ru/sites/default/files/pdf/VPK_08_476.pdf; translation downloaded from IES https://www.ies.be/files/Gerasimov%20HW%20ENG.pdf (accessed 1 January 2021).

3   Cheng, Dean. *Cyber Dragon: Inside China's Information Warfare and Cyber Operations* (Westport, CT: Praeger Security International, 2017). p. 27.

4   Ibid. p. 44 ff.

5   Ibid. p. 128.

6   Messmer, Ellen. *Serb Supporters Sock It to NATO, U.S. Web Sites* (CNN, 6 April 1999). http://edition.cnn.com/TECH/computing/9904/06/serbnato.idg/index.html (accessed 1 January 2021).

7   Tikk, Eneken, Kaska, Kadri, & Vihul, Liis. *International Cyber Incidents: Legal Considerations* (2010, pp. 18–22). https://ccdcoe.org/library/publications/international-cyber-incidents-legal-considerations/ (accessed 1 January 2021).

8   Department of Homeland Security/Cybersecurity & Infrastructure Security Agency. *Understanding Denial-of-Service Attacks* (Security Tip ST04-015. 04 November 2009). https://us-cert.cisa.gov/ncas/tips/ST04-015 (accessed 1 January 2021).

9   Emerging Technology from the arXivarchive page. *The First DDoS Attack was 20 Years Ago. This Is What We've Learned Since* (MIT Technology Review, 18 April 2019). https://www.technologyreview.com/2019/04/18/103186/the-first-ddos-attack-was-20-years-ago-this-is-what-weve-learned-since/ (accessed 1 January 2021).

10 US Department of Justice, U.S. Attorney's Office, Eastern District of New York. *Two International Cybercriminal Rings Dismantled and Eight Defendants Indicted for Causing Tens of Millions of Dollars in Losses in Digital Advertising Fraud* (27 November 2018). https://www.justice.gov/usao-edny/pr/two-international-cybercriminal-rings-dismantled-and-eight-defendants-indicted-causing (accessed 1 January 2021).

11 Haizler, Omry. The United States' Cyber Warfare History: Implications on Modern Cyber Operational Structures and Policymaking (*The Institute for National Security Studies. Cyber, Intelligence, and Security*, Vol. 1, Issue 1, January 2017). pp. 31–45. https://www.inss.org.il/he/wp-content/uploads/sites/2/systemfiles/The%20United%20States%E2%80%99%20Cyber%20Warfare%20History%20Implications%20on.pdf (accessed 1 January 2021).

12 Google Official Blog. *A New Approach to China* (12 January 2010). https://googleblog.blogspot.com/2010/01/new-approach-to-china.html (accessed 1 January 2021).

13 Sheehan, Matt. *How Google Took on China—and Lost* (MIT Technology Review, 19 December 2018). https://www.technologyreview.com/2018/12/19/138307/how-google-took-on-china-and-lost/#:~:text=Google's%20first%20foray%20into%20Chinese,over%20censorship%20of%20search%20results (accessed 1 January 2021).

14 Wadell, Kaveh. *The Computer Virus That Haunted Early AIDS Researchers* (The Atlantic, 10 May 2016). https://www.theatlantic.com/technology/archive/2016/05/the-computer-virus-that-haunted-early-aids-researchers/481965/ (accessed 1 January 2021).

15 Nakashima, Ellen & Warrick, Joby. *Stuxnet Was Work of U.S. and Israeli Experts, Officials Say* (Washington Post, 2 June 2012). https://www.washingtonpost.com/world/national-security/stuxnet-was-work-of-us-and-israeli-experts-officials-say/2012/06/01/gJQAlnEy6U_story.html (accessed 1 January 2021).

16 Greenberg, Andy. *The Untold Story of NotPetya, the Most Devastating Cyberattack in History* (Wired Magazine, 22 August 2018) https://www.wired.

com/story/notpetya-cyberattack-ukraine-russia-code-crashed-the-world/ (accessed 1 January 2021).

17 Nakashima, Ellen. *Russian Military Was Behind 'NotPetya' Cyberattack in Ukraine, CIA Concludes* (Washington Post, 13 January 2018). https://www.washington-post.com/world/national-security/russian-military-was-behind-notpetya-cyberattack-in-ukraine-cia-concludes/2018/01/12/048d8506-f7ca-11e7-b34a-b85626af34ef_story.html (accessed 1 January 2021).

18 Griffin, Andrew. *'Petya' Cyber Attack: Chernobyl's Radiation Monitoring System Hit by Worldwide Hack* (The Independent, 27 June 2017). https://www.independ-ent.co.uk/news/world/europe/chernobyl-ukraine-petya-cyber-attack-hack-nuclear-power-plant-danger-latest-a7810941.html (accessed 1 January 2021).

19 Greenberg, Andy. *The Untold Story of NotPetya, the Most Devastating Cyberattack in History* (Wired Magazine, 22 August 2018). https://www.wired.com/story/-notpetya-cyberattack-ukraine-russia-code-crashed-the-world/ (accessed 1 January 2021).

20 Borys, Christian. *Ukraine Braces for Further Cyber-Attacks* (BBC News, 25 July 2017). https://www.bbc.com/news/technology-40706093 (accessed 1 January 2021).

21 Greenberg, Andy. *Petya Ransomware Epidemic May Be Spillover From Cyberwar* (Wired Magazine, 28 June 2017). https://www.wired.com/story/petya-ransomware-ukraine/ (accessed 1 January 2021).

4

WEAPONISING ARTIFICIAL
INTELLIGENCE

All attempts to adapt our ethical code to our situation in the technological age have failed.

Max Born (1882–1970)
German physicist and a quantum mechanics pioneer

This is a chapter that is really impossible to lock down in time as new artificial intelligence techniques and tools are constantly being developed and released in what appears to be an increasing pace, and at the time of print, some aspects might already be obsolete. However, there are fundamental design tenets of the emerging generation of artificial intelligence which provide insights on what weaponised versions might look like and what they are capable of. How these can be integrated into digital warfare strategies will be discussed in this chapter, providing cues on what to expect in a near future. Now, artificial intelligence, as is intelligence itself, is hard to pin down as a concept and many of its philosophical ponderings are certainly worthy a book of its own. However, from its origins in the 1950s, it was implied that artificial intelligence would aspire to imitate the human mind and its problem-solving abilities that can be applied both to everyday and abstract situations. So, artificial intelligence originally referred to a concept known as "General Artificial Intelligence" seeking to emulate human reasoning, or even cognition. A prospect that since its inception has been easier said than done, with some questioning whether it is actually a viable quest at all. Human intelligence has so far proven to be far too versatile and flexible to be captured in code. Whilst this ambitious aspiration remains, artificial intelligence has mostly been applied on more narrow concepts of human behaviour, such as where an algorithm can help to understand speech, or identify objects or a person in an image or video. Thus, the term "artificial intelligence" is somewhat elusive, covering a broad range of items such as straightforward statistical regression techniques to the ambition of fully mimicking the human mind, and as distinct concepts are often interchangeably used, it has not alleviated the confused status of what it really means. A couple of core tenets can, however, be observed:

- Artificial intelligence is really not intelligence in the autonomous sense but rather algorithms designed to recognise patterns and from these make decisions based on set rules. For instance, stock markets have high-frequency trading bots able to dynamically adjust their automated buy and sell decisions based on changing market conditions with the objective to maximise profits without any human intervention.
- The digital transformation of pretty much everything has opened up new paths of warfare, not only from the data and systems perspectives but through the interconnects of the man–machine path as well. As business and information exchange increasingly are being conducted virtually, it is now possibly to simulate fictitious counterparts as a method to commit fraud and other cloaked malicious attacks.

For the purpose of this book, we are accepting a broad interpretation of what artificial intelligence might include, this as there are in addition a number of technical trends and principles that are augmenting its impact, even though they are not formally artificial intelligence methods. These include lowered costs and increased access to large volumes of data as well as increased computing power to facilitate the analysis. As artificial intelligence relies on creating statistical predictions and recognition of patterns, large sets of data allow for calibration and finetuning of algorithms that will be increasingly better in recognising ever more subtle and covert patterns and making decisions based on these. This enables feedback loops, and as more data get available, they can enhance the algorithms allowing them to become more powerful in their predictive capacity. In addition, the raw computing power that has become available with modern setups, such as cloud computing, has opened up possibilities to link and analyse large datasets as these can now be standardised and are cheap to use compared to only a decade ago. Thus, big data, much of which by and large are publicly available, such as in social media, can be used to improve applications and algorithms. These possibilities are obviously also applicable in digital warfare and will be decisive in forming the design features of digital weapons. This is influencing the traditional view of cyber security which has put the emphasis on two aspects:

- **Code vulnerability**. The attacker seeks to identify weak points in the code or code structure which can been exploited to gain entrance to systems for the purpose of espionage or sabotage.
- **Social engineering**. The attacker attempts through various manipulations of humans to obtain passwords or similar, or plant malware through fraudulent messages which will give them access to restricted networks and systems. It can also include operations to lure unsuspecting users into exposing confidential data or inadvertently spread viruses.

But as artificial intelligence applications are being weaponised, an additional aspect must be added, that of identifying weaknesses in various data patterns. Pattern identification as a technique is already heavily used in a number of applications, including:

- image recognition, where the technology is currently at the stage where it has become easy to recognise individual faces even in moving pictures of relatively low and blurred quality

- Natural Language Processing (NLP) that reviews human language and seeks to break down the meaning of texts into its actual concepts and tone, allowing for it to be analysed and replicated
- optimisation, such as attempting to identify the quickest, most efficient, or otherwise best route from point A to B for a huge raft of topics
- game playing algorithms that identify winning strategies within the specified rules for the particular game, such as chess or go
- anomaly or deviation detection, identifying unusual patterns that differ from the range of normality, often used to analyse financial transactions for fraudulent patterns or money laundering
- clustering techniques to find unusual and hidden patterns that cannot be intuitively identified and hypothesised by human inference, for instance used in studying consumer behaviour to identify unexpected purchasing patterns

Intrinsically linked with artificial intelligence, as being one of its key techniques, is machine learning, or the use of statistical algorithms to detect patterns and relations in data, with a view to make accurate predictions, based on training on volumes of data. Machine learning includes techniques such as Bayesian reasoning and regression analysis, classifiers like support vector machines, and predictive modelling such as decision trees. Machine learning enables the application itself, rather than a statistician or programmer, to analyse sets of data, and as applicable draws inference about any correlations that might exist in the analysed data. Whilst it can provide answers on correlation, the question of any causation is still left to human ingenuity. It generates algorithms that then can be utilised to analyse other datasets, seeking to identify similar patterns, and with access to more data it can finetune and further calibrate identified patterns. Machine-learned pattern recognition and classifications allow the use of only a few parameters to deduct more information, or to identify and group them into classes from the data they have been trained on. Deep learning is a method of machine learning that uses neural networks, which have proven to be an important method in the design of more advanced artificial intelligence applications. They are designed to mimic processes of the human brain and consist of interconnected layers of nodes, which are supposed to be the equivalent to the biological neurons, that conduct mathematical computations on inputs and then pass their result on to the next layer and so on. In that fashion, each node in the next layer receives results from the previous layer until a prediction can be made. This prediction is then compared with the expected outcome, and each connection between the nodes is adjusted and calibrated until the error between the prediction and expected outcome is minimised. "Deep" refers in short to a larger number of networks and layers being used than in typical neural networks, where, in the past, only single-layer neural networks could be handled, but with improved computing power it can be facilitated to compute several. In that sense, deep learning techniques goes above and beyond merely being a large neural network, as it also can deploy other techniques, such as comparing different regression models for best performance. Similar to the way we humans learn from mistakes, deep learning algorithms perform a task over and over, continuously making changes, ever as slight, to improve the accuracy of the outcome until it has been optimised. Some of the malware types that in the future will include these type of artificial intelligence methods are as follows:

- **Worms** are malware that by using neural networks operate by identifying target attributes such as geolocation, software, and user activity, and launch a malicious code that possesses the ability to propagate from one system to another by itself, with no human intervention. As such, it is difficult to contain as well as to eradicate an infection, as a worm is capable of both self-propagating and encrypting files as one of its "command and control" functions. By being capable of avoiding detection, through the iterative process of learning from each previous incident that they were detected in and adjust accordingly, worms can ascertain what it was that got them detected, and accordingly redesign themselves to eliminate that characteristic when preparing for the next attack. For instance, if a specific part of the code led to the detection, it can self-program to alter that particular code, or if aspects of its behaviour is being flagged by antivirus software, it could add randomness to circumvent pattern-matching rules. Famous worms, such as the aforementioned WannaCry and NotPetya, proved capable of encrypting computer files and affecting systems around the world before they were prevented and eradicated.[1,2] The next generation of worms will be enhanced so that tactics can include impersonating human interactions, operating through intelligent phishing emails, deploying machine learning or deep neural networks to conceal a ransomware attack, and will be manipulate the target system into disabling the security measures themselves.[3] Some security experts foresee that with automated self-propagation, it will be possible to infect a large number of systems while slowing down or all together avoiding detection by dynamically changing the identifiable features of the malware.[4] This type of malware can be enabled to hide itself inside other applications to reduce the risk of detection and with such evasive characteristics that it would make it challenging for defenders to identify traits that give signals of a digital attack being underway.[5]

- **Trojans** are another type of malware that create new file versions of themselves to fool detection routines. IBM Research developed DeepLocker, which was presented to the public in 2018 in a display to highlight how existing artificial intelligence methods could be combined with contemporary techniques to design a new generation of malware. It was developed with a specific stealth tactic in mind, this by avoiding detection until the moment it recognises the sought-after target and then activates. Camouflaging as a video conferencing software, DeepLocker withholds its activation until it reaches a system where a given condition is met and then it releases its malicious code. This makes the malicious code very difficult to identify and almost impossible to reverse-engineer unless one knows the activation criteria. Malware designed with these characteristics could infect many computers without being detected, only to be deployed on the intended target computers, as these are being identified by the malware. IBM highlighted DeepLocker's stealth qualities:

> It flies under the radar, avoiding detection until the precise moment it recognizes a specific target.[6]

DeepLocker uses a deep neural network model to unlock the malicious code when numerous but unique trigger conditions were met, until then it remains dormant, this not to alert antivirus software. And more importantly, DeepLocker was designed to leverage the black-box nature of the neural network to conceal what the triggering conditions were, this by ensuring that the simplistic "if this, then that" rule was transformed into a deep convolutional network of the malware code that is very hard to decipher and fathom. In addition, DeepLocker was also able to convert the concealed trigger conditions themselves into a password of sorts that is required to unlock and release it for the attack. Another malware in this category is the Emotet trojan with its main distribution mechanism being spam-phishing, usually launched through invoice scams by deceiving recipients to click on malicious email attachments. The Emotet developers did also add a component capable of stealing email data from infected victims. The purpose behind this email exfiltration capability was at first unclear, but the Emotet was observed sending out contextualised phishing emails at a large scale, meaning that it can automatically insert itself into pre-existing email threads, advising targets to click on a malicious attachment which appears in the email. This insertion technique gives the phishing email more natural context, thereby making it appear more legitimate. Thus, an attack of this type can be "super charged" by customising the email content, such as through deploying less standardised language, enabled by an ability to learn and replicate natural language by analysing the context of the individual email threads. These phishing emails could become highly tailored to individuals by using jargon and slang to create and insert entirely bespoke and credible emails, individualised in millions, which would increase their success rate considerably.[7]

- **Deepfakes**, a mix of the phrases "deep learning" and "fake media," is going to have a huge effect on digital weapons, and it is currently best understood by looking at automated chatbots that use natural language processing software, sometimes referred to as trolls. They operate by sending out messages, trying to act human by using "normal" language on various social media but have so far generally been so crude that distinguishing them from real humans is rarely a major problem. But improved artificial intelligence algorithms are starting to change all that, making these bots harder and harder to detect. There are already algorithms able to analyse a person's use of language, choice of words, and tone-of-voice and then reasonably convincingly impersonate that individual if given enough data. The end goals for groups with criminal intent is to be able to generate emails or messages targeting specific individuals and convincing them the sender is a genuine person, even someone they already have an established relationship with. More spectacular, is that it already now is possible to produce relatively convincing fake videos and audio, bringing deepfakes to a sinister new level that have become so authentic that even through a professional review they can at times appear authentic, and likely convince at least some targets of the genuine intent of their message.

In 2019, Samsung's Moscow-based Artificial Intelligence Laboratory released a deepfake of an unusually high quality. It had been developed through the use of generative adversarial network (GAN). GANs feature two competing neural networks. One network, called a generator, prepares a feature based on a real image. It then shows that feature to the other network, called the discriminator, that determines if this image is real or fake. As the images are created, then judged, the reproduction's realism improves proportionately to the discriminator's decreasing ability to determine what is real or not. The power of this machine learning technique is that it can be trained to generate moving images from just one single image. Computer vision techniques, like focal point identification, can be coupled with GANs to track a specific object in an image or video. Previous methods required hundreds of thousands of images, usually from individual frames of video to train a model to mimic an individual face, but this particular model required no more than 16 images, and with more different angles of the face the more seamlessly it can replicate the targeted individual. This algorithm uses specific facial features, identifying the eyes, the nose, the mouth, and the jawline for a meta training phase of the model. Once these movements are understood by the GAN, it can overlay new images in a realistic manner. The algorithm only requires images of such quality that can be easily acquired through social media or surveillance of the targeted individual.[8]

A tool called StyleGAN by Nvidia enables the generation of synthetic portraits by utilising a computer vision technique known as style transfer. StyleGAN can transfer characteristics of one individual to another, to make a completely unique, synthetic image. As built, it can change high-level attributes, such as the pose or identity of a person, to low-level ones, including hair length and colour and skin features in its generation process. It is a useful technique in creating more authentic online persons where social media campaigns rely on specifically programmed bots to push narratives into the public's forefront. Through StyleGAN, robust and unique profiles can be created using synthetically generated images, which are tweaked to fit the pose or characteristics of a real person, something which some claim already maybe happening.[9] GANs have also been applied to text generation, and Russia is known to have deployed thousands of twitter bots to conduct influencing campaigns, although most of them easily recognisable as such.

Augmented by facial landmark tracking, which identifies specific features of a face, it allows the program to accurately swap the target face. Similar technologies already exist on sites like

Instagram and SnapChat in the form of face swapping and filters. An algorithm is then able to match the mouth and face to
synchronise with spoken words. The end result is essentially a
face-swap: splicing a person's head onto another person's body
with near undetectable changes. Researchers at Taiwan National
University modified a GAN tool, labelled *CycleGAN*, to create more
a reliable sentiment compared to the typical *Seq2Seq* method currently employed in chatbots. This improvement, when coupled
with the coherence and semantics of Seq2Seq, can create realistic
chatbots, giving responses in real time that closely resemble those
of a human. This allows for greater coverage of social media spaces
and the distribution of messages within those domains. Adversarial attacks on text data, such as gradual changes to invalid words or
changes of word sequence, can ultimately alter the actual semantic meaning of a text, conveying an altogether different message.[10]
Improvements to audio synthesis, particularly of human voices,
are also a cause for concern. Adobe Voco and Google Deepmind's
WaveGAN can currently copy an individual's voice with as little
as 40 minutes of audio, matching vocalisations of words not even
spoken. With these emerging technologies acting in concert and
aiming for perfection in impersonating a human, a targeted victim, who really could be anyone, is at the mercy of the deep fake's
creator, who can use the technology to fabricate various compromising scenes, such as of a pornographic nature or a crime,
and dubious claims could be made by corrupt law enforcements
as pretext for arrests and incarcerations with deepfakes as evidence. Fabricated videos can now be produced that provoke and
stir social unrests with a view of triggering spontaneous violence.
Deepfakes can also be used in incredibly convincing spear phishing attacks that users would be hard-pressed to identify as false. As
attacks get more personalised, even the most security-aware user
might be exploited, and exposed personal data have already been
used in extortion scams to fool users into paying large sums to an
acclaimed hacker who supposedly has video proof of lewd sexual
acts, for instance.

So far mostly part of science fiction novels but a long-time aspiration of generalised artificial intelligence is to have applications that can learn to act themselves, something that can be hinted at in the form of unsupervised machine learning. As an example, a Twitter bot that was based on unsupervised machine learning had to be taken offline rather quickly when it started imitating unbecoming human behaviour, including profanities, that it had learned from Twitter users. In essence, it was becoming humanlike but not in the intended manner. This was an eerie example of how easily machine learning applications can imitate an undesired version of reality when left without human supervision.

But for now, pattern seeking algorithms still largely need human initiation and intervention, coding them with what, when, and how to commence the search for patterns and on what data types in accordance to pre-set criteria. What has speeded up much of the artificial intelligence revolution is that programming code now can be recycled to a greater extent than previously. This means that new algorithms less often have to be written from scratch but through open-source facilities, existing code can be reused, albeit typically customised for the bespoke purpose. Thus, much of the core code in several artificial intelligence applications are now publicly accessible. It means that algorithms that only a decade ago were available to only researchers and hard for others to access, seen as proprietary intellectual property, are now almost instantly available to anyone writing applications or software. Being able to leverage these open sources, malware developers and security experts to greatly advance viruses and antiviruses in a cycle of attacks and counterattacks. Hackers are combining open-source code with add-ons and bespoke adjustments to create malware. These can be used to conceal malware that has been embedded in seemingly standard applications where the malicious behaviour of the code is not triggered until the application reaches a particular target. The code is often controlled through a private key that serves as the trigger to determine the time and place of unlocking and releasing the hidden malware. For instance, as discussed in Chapter 3, in the attacks on Estonia and

Ukraine, the malware developers did not write much code themselves but combined code and tools available on the dark web and used it to attack known weaknesses. This highlights one strong point of artificial intelligence, its ability to adapt to a new environment or to use knowledge acquired from past incidents. So, algorithms can be made capable of learning and retaining what worked during an attack and how to circumvent deterrents. They can be made resilient to withstand failed attempts to penetrate and adjusted to be successful in ensuing attacks. And they could also self-propagate once inside a computer network, as they are developed for a more indiscriminate search for security vulnerabilities with its dynamic capabilities making it hard to foresee the damage they might create, hence it acts opportunistic, using a raft of attack possibilities. With the increased speed ever faster, everywhere, it is creating ad hoc networks that are harder to secure and easier to exploit, opening up for swarm-based attacks where individual applications or elements of code perform a specific function as part of a larger and coordinated attack. As and when one incorporates artificial intelligence algorithms into a network of connected devices that can communicate, these devices can not only launch attacks on their own but customise the attacks on the go based on what they learn during the attacks facilitated – an intelligent cluster of bots that can share information and learn from each other in real time. By incorporating these self-learning technologies, it becomes possible to create attacks capable of quickly assessing vulnerabilities and then apply methods of countering efforts to prevent them.

In summary, the emerging generation of artificial intelligence brings with it a number of features, and we can already notice the influence of some in the design of digital weapons:

- **Big data**. Whilst the access to big data is not in itself artificial intelligence, it has provided the material to develop algorithms on and is becoming the battle ground for digital warfare. As so much more data can now be stored and utilised, previously unknown patterns can be identified and used for attacks.

- **Machine learning/automated coding**. It has come to define much of what today is understood as artificial intelligence, in essence, through statistical modelling identify patterns in data, and from it provide predictive analytics, typically based on correlation rather than causation. The main characteristic of machine learning is that it seeks to identify patterns and rules in a set of data and these will generate algorithms rather than the programmer formulating it. For instance, filters to identify spam were previously coded by programmers that included rules to define inappropriate emails if they contain certain keywords or phrases. Nowadays, supervised machine learning would from a set of identified spam emails seek out patterns, of which some are likely not to have been recognised by humans, such as a broader set of vocabulary, number of recipients, or source of origin, and from these findings, without human intervention, develops a statistically validated algorithm that can distinguish spam from legitimate messages.

- **Impersonations of humans**. Digital warfare attacks are increasingly being customised, targeting the idiosyncrasies of every identified opponent, and yet able to operate at scale. Nuances can be identified and mimicked, such as a particular individual's behaviour and language, this by analysing emails and social media communications. Malware developers will be able to use this knowledge to replicate a user's writing style, crafting messages that appear highly credible, to the point of being impossible to distinguish from genuine communication. Online correspondence, be it emails or messages, will for the foreseeable future remain the insertion point of malware, leaving very few systems entirely ringfenced. The imitation of human activity online is facilitated through the enormous amount of digital traces we are leaving that highlights both patterns we are aware of and perhaps more interesting ones we are not. These can be traced through most digital outlets. In all, it will often be possible to establish a social profile highlighting preferences, likes and dislikes, language, frequencies, timing, and other habitual patterns, which all can be replicated, and then can form the basis to create fake identities and develop "Deepfakes" indistinguishable from individuals.

- **Autonomous agents – blending into the background**. Sophisticated digital warriors aspire to ensure that their malware maintains a long-term presence in their target environments without being detected. They operate with caution to evade traditional security checks and controls and are often uniquely designed to target specific organisations, even individuals. These artificial intelligence-infused malwares will also be able to learn how to function covertly and efficiently in the prevalent communication channels, identifying the best ports and protocols to use to move around inside a system and seeking to discretely blending in with routine activity. This ability to disguise itself and hide amid the commonplace noise will mean that malware is able to covertly spread within a digital environment, and stealthily compromise more devices than ever before. Such malware will also be able to analyse vast volumes of data at machine speed, rapidly identifying which data sets are valuable and which are not and decide what action to take. This will save the developer of malicious code a great deal of time and effort when supervising and executing an attack.

- **Faster attacks with more detrimental consequences**. Currently, the most sophisticated malware attacks require skilled developers and social engineers to conduct research on their target and identify individuals of interest, understand their social media connections and networks, and observe over time how they interact on digital platforms. With this emerging technology, an offensive artificial intelligence algorithm will be able to achieve a level of sophistication in a fraction of that time, and at scale. Not only will such attacks be much more tailored and consequently more effective, the malwares' ability to understand context means they will be even harder to detect. Traditional security controls will be impotent against this new threat, as they can only spot predictable and pre-modelled activity. And as malware are constantly evolving, they will become ever-more resistant to the categorisation of threats that remains fundamental to the modus operandi of legacy security approaches.

By applying the framework introduced in Chapter 3, with its six steps, the structure of a digital attack with the described emerging artificial intelligence applications and methods can better be depicted and elaborated as below.

THE RECONNAISSANCE PHASE

During the reconnaissance phase, the ambition of the attacker is to figure out which systems and networks the target uses and what their technical as well as human vulnerabilities might be. It is a phase where both public and semi-public information are combined and ascertained with analytics to identify potentially exploitable patterns and get a clearer picture of the presumed battlefield. Hence, the reconnaissance phase takes aim at two vectors.

One is the collation of human intelligence, which, amongst others tasks, includes tapping into an individual's social media activities, with a view to identify potential peculiarities, and determining key personnel in targeted corporations with authorisation over certain systems of interest or likely to have access to confidential information. This can be done through collating career-related information on platforms such as LinkedIn and similar. It can also include gathering information from discussion forums on what network and systems that particular organisations are using. This type of intelligence exercise has been greatly facilitated as it is currently close to impossible for any corporation or its employees to operate without leaving any form of digital traces. So, the rise of social networks and big data have improved the opportunities for researching human and organisational targets that might be susceptible to blackmailing or illicit extraction of information. Open social networks that can be screened and scraped for content, including preferences, relationships, and the style and tone of language that the targets use in various contexts, are information that is typically gathered. Or data of a more intimate nature can of course be stolen and analysed for habitual patterns, and possibly combined with other covertly obtained data to help create psychological and social profiles of potential targets. Gathering and then categorising and analysing this data would have been a very time-consuming exercise previously, but by utilising automated tools, these can facilitate the identification and recognition of patterns that the target himself might not be fully aware of, and which are then susceptible for fraudulent exploits or replication. Pattern recognition algorithms could target groups based on political inclination through tracing vocabulary and phrases common for certain political views (such as left-wing, right-wing) or advocates for specific agendas (environment, religious) and specifically only attacking these individuals, and not others, with malware, seeking to intimidate them or otherwise harass them.

The other vector is the more traditional hacker method of illicitly gaining access to systems to gather intelligence. As for computer systems and networks, artificial intelligence can help detect patterns on how data travels to and from the open internet, and together with reviewing the metadata that systems leave behind, it will be possible to identify what software and platforms that a target utilises as well as when and how. Once again, analysing this is a complicated and time-consuming process for a human operator, but equipped with the latest artificial intelligence applications and the now low-cost of handling data will make this a much easier endeavour than before.

Artificial intelligence applications can also be deployed to search for targets through predictive analytics, thereby increasing the opportunities for attacks. In marketing, algorithms are already standard as a means to identify potential customers, where thousands of factors are analysed to time and calibrate the content of promotional activities.

THE WEAPONISATION PHASE

Set goal ➤ Recon ➤ Weaponize ➤ Intrusion ➤ Exploit/Expand ➤ Command ➤ Act ➤ Disguise

Whilst the work of writing code and combining toolkits will mostly remain a human task, as more advanced artificial intelligence tools become available and easier to combine, modify, and use, the arsenal for a malicious actor will be greatly enhanced. This also includes the open-source artificial intelligence code libraries that will lower the cost and increase the possibilities to design more powerful malware with less requirements of advanced coding capabilities and other human inputs. With more advanced reconnaissance tactics, additional information can be gathered about the targeted individual and his behaviour. Better intelligence allows for an improved ability to predict what security the weaponised code might encounter and need to circumvent. This knowledge and behavioural patterns gathered can be used to create algorithms that automate and predict the security arrangements it must defeat. Through continuous testing protocols, risks can be detected by combining different toolkits based on specific system setups and security software, such as the previously described GAN. The design of malware through such customised varieties can then be applied for bespoke attacks of such a sophistication level that a human could likely be able to develop. This sophistication can also be augmented by applying polymorphic code, where it can recognise what system it is running in and adapt the code to appear safe and not be detected. As a simple example, a block of code might be able to figure out that it is running on a designer computer, this as it has designer software installed, and rewrite itself and its functionality to resemble code coming from Adobe to avoid detection. The code can be altered as "if *photoshop_installed=true then rename_to_AdobePlugin*" by utilising a polymorphic approach altering it dynamically, thereby making it harder to detect and more efficient in its intrusion attempts.

With more advanced testing and access to raw computing power, it will open up the possibility to more efficiently and through automating many of its steps seek to find zero-exploits and bugs in various systems source code, in particular if these have been made publicly available. Algorithms can basically scan the source code and by comparing it with other publicly available code aspire to identify weaknesses, either previously known or unknown, that can be exploited for intrusion. And as many standard systems and networks increasingly provide open-source code, which typically can be copied from generally available code libraries, it is increasingly possible to identify more precisely how, when, and why it is being used by a target. Based with such knowledge, specifically designed algorithms can be infused to beef up malware to automatically be able to seek out exploitable weaknesses that provide a potential path to illicit access.

THE INTRUSION PHASE

The intrusion phase means getting the malicious code into the target's computer or system. The obvious use of artificial intelligence here is in combination with the information acquired, accumulated, and analysed in the reconnaissance phase, but there are also other potential tactics that can be considered. The algorithms might also utilise pattern recognition and learning from failures to seek to overcome security systems that track and alert unusual traffic and data patterns.

A currently used as well as simple method to covertly install a malware on a system or network is to deceive users to click on email attachments. Obviously, if it comes across as too apparently fraudulent or seen as merely spam, then it will quickly be discovered and deleted, often the content of the email fails to resonate with the designated recipient. But with more advanced language models, notably specialised natural language processing tools, these can be used to generate text that more closely resemble conversations in specific social media groups or use bespoke corporate jargon, thus appearing to be a post or email from an actual human, which will increase the chance that a targeted individual will respond favourably and download suspicious data or documents containing malicious code. It also means the initial attack might not include the malware, but a first attempt is made to entice and lure the user to reply to some specific questions that an algorithm calculates that the user might react positively to with a view to deliver the malicious coder later in the corresponding chain of conversation, as trust has been established. This is an approach that will further reduce the risk of being discovered, like that of embedding the malware through distributing emails *en masse* and then hoping to deceive as many as possible. Thus, a targeted attack with a specifically designed language by specially crafted fake profiles will improve the likelihood for success than relying on emails with a generic language from an unfamiliar source.

Intelligent agents with the capacity to dynamically respond to new information and pattern recognition tools are making it possible to reduce the need for programmers and hackers to through an automated approach constantly be on the search for weaknesses and seek out the most promising vector attacks. By collating and analysing these weaknesses, they can help to form strategies, which will be unique for each target and then much harder to defend against. With the introduction of deepfake audio and video, a senior executive can be imitated, calling up and ordering a junior employee to install a certain software or open an email attachment and thereby infiltrate the network.

Today, many systems are developed on a number of open-source components, established on the principle that anyone can access and read the code with a view to improve it to remove bugs, or use parts of the code for other applications. There is a huge library of code on GitHub, where a lot of organisations simply without any greater security scrutiny utilise the modules made available and sometimes modify them for their internal systems. The open-source architecture with all its advantages obviously also comes with significant security vulnerabilities, hence by identifying potential security exploits in particular code sequences, such as in the GitHub library, an attacker can, through code recognition tools, scan internal systems for code with similar structure, code that relies on a module block with a known weakness, or code that has simply been copied straight from a module, and exploit them.

THE EXPLOIT/EXPAND PHASE

Once able to access the inside of a network, the attackers' goal is often to spread throughout it, hide the malware as necessary and identify what data to steal or seek to find further vulnerable systems to attack. As described in the Stuxnet case, the attackers had designed a highly sophisticated intrusion method that specifically targeted a particular system, but in the NotPetya case, the attack was much broader in scope, attempting to infect as many computers and systems as possible, seeking to create maximum damage, but thereby carrying the risk of being detected at an early stage. Artificial intelligence tools create new opportunities to improve the efficiency of digital attacks, where more targeted strikes and case-by-case methods can be used to increase precision. An autonomous agent can be trained to recognise a system only by a few variables, and equipped with that knowledge, deduct what method to use (if not included in the original package download) and attack specific weaknesses while being more covert, and also be able to opt to not attack where there are security applications they may not manage to circumvent. Pattern recognition techniques make it possible to hide malicious code and replicate normal usage patterns for the network, therefore making it far harder to discover the threat which might be able to stay in hiding for a longer time. Artificial intelligence-induced bots will also be able to improve current methods by identifying, recognising, and selecting likely high-worth targets in terms of data possession or financial means for blackmailing purposes and further reducing risk of being discovered by not bothering to scan useless data or attack targets of a perceived lower value. As previously mentioned in the weaponising phase, artificial intelligence can also be used to analyse patterns and behaviour of other applications, this to enhance an autonomous agent's ability to identify if it should stay covert or adapt by using suitable polymorphic code. All these capabilities represent a huge workload for a human team and require a raft of skillsets to be able to dig through system logs to identify applications with potential weaknesses and adjust the malware that enables them to penetrate through these security gaps and stay inactive until the most valuable targets have been identified. So, by identifying likely system configurations and settings, and covertly monitoring network traffic, artificial intelligence-enabled virus or malware can choose a mode of attack, avoid paths where there is a higher degree of likelihood of being detected, and focus on less-supervised infiltration points. By aligning with the regular network traffic and its frequencies, the malware seeks to blend in so its communication will not stand out as deviating and raise suspicion. Hence, part of the attack strategy will be to collate information on the characteristics of the network traffic – the how, the when, and the who – and then identify the lowest risk of communication as per the timing, content, and format of a message. The algorithm will therefore target not to become an anomaly vis-à-vis its operating environment.

THE COMMAND PHASE

In the command and control phase, the goal is to enable communication with the inserted malicious code to either decide when to strike, when to go into (or remain in) hiding, or when to extract and send out data. The control and command of the malware is often the most risky phase of a digital attack, as data typically is sent to external servers that are not known to the system administrators. The illicit extraction of data is an uncertain undertaking as transferring or even storing large amounts of data will carry the risk of detection by the unusual data patterns it typically leaves behind, which can be detected through standard security measures. Pattern recognition can help to figure out how the target's systems normally communicate, thereby identifying deviations it should avoid. It can record if a user is submitting messages to strange and anonymous email addresses or obscure websites, it can detect if users are requesting a specific service, such as cloud storage systems, including at what time and if it connects to the command systems in a manner that seems similar to making ordinary calls, as a strategy to stay hidden. One advantage over current command and control systems is that autonomous agents are able to make decisions on their own. This will reduce the need for a centralised control and command function that either becomes altogether obsolete, or that the autonomous agents can themselves decide how and where to communicate with the central command, enabling it to much more efficiently hide and avert detection, rather than operating in a pre-set, standardised manner. This is making malware far more difficult to detect and remove, and combined with polymorphic code, it will allow for viruses that can spread and infect on their own, acting laterally or going into hiding, and so on. But the risk is overwhelming that these can become malwares running amok, difficult to get rid of, and, as they are continuously evolving, leading to a generation of malware that is far more destructive than current versions.

THE ACT PHASE

The act phase is quite hard to define as it depends on the initially set goals, be it either stealing data, performing an act of sabotage, or executing any other action aligned with the particular goal. One scenario that has not yet materialised but certainly is possible, is to utilise artificial intelligence algorithms against targets that themselves rely on artificial intelligence algorithms, and poisoning the input data used by the opponent's machine learning tools with the goal of alter decision-making towards the preferred goals of the attacker. The objective is to contaminate datasets or circumvent the logic that artificial intelligence-based systems use to drive it towards erroneous algorithms. This could also include manipulating text messages by changing the content for the attacker's advantageous direction.

Essentially, this opens up an avenue of not only destroying data, or hardware as the Stuxnet virus was able to do, but directly influencing the decisions of the opponents by tampering with their business model that relies on certain sets of data. Artificial intelligence-augmented malware will thus be able to strike with a greater precision through significantly sharpened penetrating and destructive characteristics.

In summary, the enablement of artificial intelligence will allow malware to act more humanlike and in that sense provide more precision in the attacks as, for instance, it will be better in understanding natural human language and thereby able to generate bespoke messages containing the malware. It is also able to operate on a scale through automation that humans are not able to by significantly increasing not only the number of attacks but also the type of attacks, including data breaches, extortion operations, destruction and disruption attacks, and repurpose attacks circumventing the need for a corresponding number of humans involved. The highlights of some of the suggested artificial intelligence methods and tools along the attack chain are given in the following table.

Reconnaissance	Weaponise	Intrusion	Exploit/Expand	Command & Control	Act	Disguise
Intelligence gathering & analytics, incl human intelligence& systems Selection of most promising targets Vulnerability detection Learn target standard behaviour	Attack planning Attack code generation Classifier manipulation	Phishing & spear phishing Password attacks Captcha attacks	Network & system mapping Network behaviour analysis	Domain generation Self-learning malware Swarm-based command & control	Self-learning malware NLP manipulation	Obfuscation techniques to avoid discovery

NOTES

1 Svensson, Erik, Magnusson, Jonas, & Zuave, Erik. *Kryptomaskar och deras konsekvenser Åtgärder för cybersäkerhet utifrån fallen WannaCry och NotPetya* (FOI-R--4774--SE ISSN 1650-1942, FOI, June 2019).

2 Fruhlinger, Josh. *What is WannaCry Ransomware, How Does It Infect, and Who Was Responsible?* (CSO, 30 August 2018). https://www.csoonline.com/article/3227906/what-is-wannacry-ransomware-how-does-it-infect-and-who-was-responsible.html (accessed 1 January 2021).

3 Lando, Gabriel. *Machine Vs. Machine. A Look at AI-powered Ransomware* (FileCloud Blog, 27 August 2018). https://www.getfilecloud.com/blog/2018/08/-machine-vs-machine-a-look-at-ai-powered-ransomware/#.X-McsthKg2w (accessed 1 January 2021).

4 Rhode, B. (ed.). Artificial Intelligence and Offensive Cyber Weapon (*Strategic Comments*, Vol. 25, Issue 10 (2019)).

5 Stoecklin, Marc Ph. *DeepLocker: How AI Can Power a Stealthy New Breed of Malware* (Security Intelligence, 8 August 2018). https://securityintelligence.com/-deeplocker-how-ai-can-power-a-stealthy-new-breed-of-malware/ (accessed 1 January 2021).

6 Ibid.

7 Cybersecurity & Infrastructure Security Agency. *Alert (AA20-280A) Emotet Malware* (National Cyber Awareness System, 6 October 2020). https://us-cert.cisa.gov/ncas/alerts/aa20-280a (accessed 1 January 2021).

8 Barber, Gregory. *Deepfakes Are Getting Better, But They're Still Easy to Spot* (Wired, 26 May 2019). https://www.wired.com/story/deepfakes-getting-better-theyre-easy-spot/ (accessed 1 January 2021).

9 Satter, Raphael. *Experts: Spy Used AI-Generated Face to Connect with Targets* (New York: Associated Press, 13 June 2019). https://apnews.com/article/bc2f19097a4c4fffaa00de6770b8a60d (accessed 1 January 2021).

10 Hosseini-Asl, Ehsan, Zhou, Yingbo, Xiong, Caiming, & Socher, Richard. *A Multi-Discriminator CycleGAN for Unsupervised Non-Parallel Speech Domain Adaptation* (Salesforce Research, 9 July 2018). https://arxiv.org/pdf/1804.00522.pdf (accessed 1 January 2021).

5

BLITZKRIEG IN THE
DIGITAL AGE

Frieden zu sichern ist die Vorbereitung für Krieg
To secure peace is to prepare for war.

Carl von Clausewitz (1780–1831) legendary
German war strategist

What would Clausewitz have thought of digital warfare that uses technologies that only 20 years ago was hard to fathom, let alone during his lifetime two centuries ago? In his writings, Clausewitz never really concerned himself much with the technological development of arms, something that he must have at least considered being in the midst of an enormous pace of innovation in those early years of industrialisation. Or did he simply see through all that, insightfully realising that it was not so much the capacity and capabilities of the weapons that decided the outcome of battles but the human intentions behind them? We previously noted that whilst the world's superpowers together hold gigantic nuclear arsenals, they have become politically impossible to put into action. A realisation that dawned almost immediately after the first two atomic bombs were dropped over Hiroshima and Nagasaki in August of 1945. Now nuclear weapons are, much like in the prisoner's dilemma conundrum, mostly stored and maintained simply because potentially rivalling countries also are storing and maintaining them. It does seems that human intent still matters and as our psychological make-up has not changed much in 200 years, and probably not even in 2,000 years, analysing digital warfare from a Clausewitzian perspective should have merit and provide a valuable historical perspective on the future of warfare. But what is new is that the emergence of a digital sphere has created a completely new dimension and a new delivery mechanism that increases speed, reach, stealth, precision, diffusion, and the breath of an attack, this as the digital world increasingly is becoming the world that matters. Even if there arguably has not yet been an example of a full-scale digital war, there are already several incidents providing highlights of what can be expected, being part of hybrid warfare strategies that typically include several digital aspects:

- They are built around a diversity of tools, mostly of non-military, non-lethal characteristics.
- They tend to operate under anonymity or through proxy groups, making attribution difficult.
- Data or information is increasingly being used as ammunition, where the ability to influence perceptions can be decisive.
- Psychological warfare is used to exploit and seek to create social, religious, political, ethnical, or other divisions among the opponents.
- So-called shocking truths, even when they actually are lies, are used to create immediate shock effects that will effectively disarm an opponent, temporarily at least, and put him on the defence.
- Digital tools and social media operations are integrated into the overall strategy to accelerate and compound impacts.
- The data patterns we advertently and inadvertently leave behind us is becoming a new battlefield.
- Economic pressures can be applied to reinforce the severity of the attacks.
- There has been an increased use of intelligence in both offensive and defensive purposes to craft more precise strategies.

The targets in a hybrid conflict will at times be of a "pawn sacrifice" type, such as smaller states in the vicinity of greater powers that are being singled out to fall under their dominance. This scenario will also apply to affiliated corporations attacked either directly or being hit as collateral damage. This can extend to basically any proxy targets used to threaten the main adversaries, typically of an economic nature. They will be considered easy prey in that they will often lack the capability to defend themselves properly and are unlikely to retaliate. Therefore, the capacity and willingness to use conventional weapons will still play a role, as attacking a country with an impressive arsenal and a trigger-happy pedigree will be an opponent that might not satisfy itself with a digital eye-to-eye response but might seek to go after its enemies "in real life." Thus, an aggressor needs to factor in not only the likelihood of retaliation but what form it might take. The previously described attacks against Estonia and Ukraine are applicable cases in point on how a vastly more powerful nation, in this case Russia being singled out as the culprit, will strike against its smaller neighbours with little risk of repercussions. For the weaker part, one of the few viable strategies will be to make sure that they always run faster than other potential victims by having the most resilient defence, or forming alliances with stronger nations, so they might be the ones let off the hook, as there are easier targets to go after. The aggressors, unlike conventional warfare, will cover a wide range from nation states to criminal groups, hacktivists, and maybe even the disgruntled but resourceful individual. At times these will be working in cahoots, based on the notion that the enemies' enemy is my friend regardless of rationale, and will in varying degrees be able to launch highly destructive digital attacks that could come to also claim human lives. The highlight of this chapter is the pragmatic realisation that the digital battlefield will overwhelmingly involve corporations, either as proxy targets or direct targets, and that it is now business critical that they understand the digital war strategies, of which some have links back to Clausewitz. Referring to blitzkrieg is apt as it is what defines many of these strategies: fast execution, a mixture of digital tools enhanced through artificial intelligence to maximise the detrimental effects, and a heavy emphasis on psychological warfare to create shock. The schwerpunkts will, as a general rule, be of an abstract nature, such as targeting a corporation's brand, directly or indirectly, which as a consequence might spell its commercial demise. As some digital attacks, such as shutting down power grids, do hold the propensity to cause bodily harm, intentionally or not, they should therefore fall under the definition of war proper. As previously described, that notion is supported by the insight that they are often backed by the threat of use of conventional weapons should matters escalate in particular when nation states are involved. However, given the digital armoury's largely non-lethal characteristics and that the number of "traditional" wars have diminished, the objective of digital conflicts, much to Clausewitz's point, still do share the ultimate objective of how he defined war, namely, to conquer by breaking an opponent's will, but in this context not necessarily having to bash the enemy's head in. In a sense, digital warfare both accentuates and reduces war. The point some are making that we now are in an ongoing state of conflict is certainly valid, but it is bloodless and many do rarely notice much of it, typically being conducted anonymously and covertly, and even at its worse it generally merely includes a temporary shutdown of an internet connection, online banking services no longer working, or a power grid closed down. Nuisances, yes sure, but they typically never last longer than a few hours and then normality returns. It means that the world has entered an era marked by a constant noise of low-level conflicts, typically going on behind the scenes and against proxy targets, however with the propensity to at times break out into full scale war.

An aggressor has essentially two core strategies to choose from as a means to subjugate an opponent: the first one is seeking to eliminate the capacity (or more likely psychological willpower) to defend himself by undermining the resistance to reject hostile demands. The other is to inflict such high costs or economic or political pain, or sometimes merely presenting the capability to do so, that an opponent is willing to negotiate an end to hostilities, or the threats thereof, on the terms desired. The first of these alternatives represents what has traditionally been called a *strategy of annihilation*, in which the (military) objective is unlimited, a scenario Clausewitz pointed out that for political reasons rarely is viable; however, in the digital warfare context annihilation takes on a different meaning: targeting corporates in particular basically means seeking to take them out of business, and perhaps permanently so. Typically, a strategy of annihilation is only possible when a combatant possesses a great superiority over the enemy, in terms of brute strength, military skill, leadership, technological capabilities, or morale. The second strategy option is referred to as a *strategy of erosion*, in which the (military) objective is limited, as a crushing and decisive strike might not be possible, instead making sure that the opponent's costs of defending himself become so high that he will find ending the war on the opponent's terms more attractive than commencing or continuing to fight. Often an aggressor's superiority lies in surprise (read: blitzkrieg-style attacks), which from the digital warfare perspective becomes an enticing proposition, if the attacker can find vulnerabilities of a schwerpunkt character and through stealth with a successful strike obliterate the opponent from operating, even from existing. A blitzkrieg approach can share elements of both the aforementioned strategies, by seeking to quickly annihilate a schwerpunkt, this through efficiently shutting down a system or online service that render a business model out of action, which can at the same time, if the opponent becomes shocked enough by the surprise, quickly erode a resilient attitude towards defence and potential retaliation. A possible outcome, if achieved through a one-off single blow and facilitated by a psychological warfare operation, can result in a *fait accompli*, an accomplished consequence that simply cannot be undone; in this perspective it could mean the bankruptcy or takeover of a corporation. The objective is to publicly highlight the defender's weakness; its credibility and business model might have become so impaired that any recovery is not possible, for the short-term at least.

Clausewitz argued that defence was superior to an offensive strategy, but does that claim also hold true in digital wars? In a conventional war, the defender can benefit from fighting on home soil and from the attacker eventually suffering from inadequate supply lines, but how does that translate in a digital setting? Superficially, it might appear that the attacker holds all the strong cards, as he can chose when and how to, for instance, plant a malware; it is cheap, relatively simple to execute, it can be done anonymously, and it is difficult for a defender to pre-empt other than with the standard antivirus software and similar. However, unlike conventional warfare, digital weapons are often characterised by "use or lose" capabilities, which means once an attack has been executed, the specific malware can only occasionally be used again, as antivirus software and other security tools will prevent and neutralise them as the method and sometimes also the code become publicly known, essentially rendering them useless for future deployment. As they become unworkable, an attacker might run out of digital fire power and a continuation of the conflict will require access to other weapons, hence a warfare strategy must be carefully crafted and is likely to become a hybrid conflict or simply end by fizzling out. What is more is that if standard antivirus software packages get upgraded to offset the specific malicious code used, its deployment on other potential targets will also be prevented. Thus, an attack can only commence if security vulnerabilities are identified, a proposition far from certain, which means that intent is not enough, but it will ultimately hinge on technical competence of both opponents. A successful defence strategy will therefore be focused on making sure that the initial attack is either all together diverted, or through robust defence mechanism the damages are minimised without severely affecting the brand, systems, or operations.

Creativity and capability in developing malware and resilient safety measures against them will therefore largely decide the outcome, and more than in conventional warfare, quality will precede quantity, essentially a single highly skilful hacker will be able to defeat a large number of average or mediocre counterhackers or security experts. Hence, the success, and even the possibility, of a war depends on the access to highly competent creative digital soldiers, applying a "brains before brawns" approach. From that perspective, an aggressor will have the advantage of surprise only if he is sure of penetrating identified vulnerabilities and if the assault is capable of causing so severe damage that they will take out schwerpunkts and damage them beyond a quick fix. This as an offensive can quickly fade if the malware is eliminated, data and services restored, and if an enemy is not able to constantly reinvent his arsenal of digital weapons. So, if a defender manages to quickly plug security gaps and neutralise the malware, an attack is bound to fizzle out as known vulnerabilities are exhausted, and the advantage has then shifted to the defender, an aspect which still makes Clausewitz's premise hold true.

The Clausewitzian trinity will also apply in the digital context with psychological warfare seeking to entice *passions* through influencing campaigns; deep fakes can come to be utilised to produce sensations that manage to stir up the required emotions. There is a *rationality* behind the objectives set which could be political or outright economics, weighing these against the risks of detection and retaliation. Finally, the creative, or in Clausewitz's terms *irrational*, part, perhaps more important now than in traditional warfare, which seeks to overcome digital frictions by identifying and circumventing vulnerabilities and security gaps. However, dangers exist as unlike conventional warfare, computer systems are nowadays so highly interconnected that it is not always possible to foresee any collateral damages that might also interrupt unintended targets, such as a virus starting to spread and infecting external systems, creating unforeseeable frictions that also might impact the attacker.

AN ANATOMY OF DIGITAL ATTACKS

The CHAOS acronym presented in Chapter 3 is a method to provide a guideline on how an aggressor typically structures a digital assault in its broadest sense, and with the emerging artificial intelligence techniques each component of this acronym will be accentuated.

- **Cheap**. Low-cost code sequences and readily available tools from a raft of libraries, such as GitHub, as well as testing of data now being much more accessible are making the development of digital weapons much more viable, covering a broader range of capabilities. It is now easier than before to detect patterns, in particular to perform analysis on social media data, where the opportunities to conduct fraudulent activities has increased significantly. This provides a whole new prospective of armoury that can be enabled and the number of potential digital warriors with a sinister intent of causing destruction is manifold.

- **Hit-and-run**. The increased use of social media and other platforms have made it easier to weaponise and exploit security vulnerabilities in applications, networks, and systems of corporations and individual users alike. Observations have already been made on how artificial intelligence tools are used to exploit the weaknesses inherent in human nature, in particular rules-of-thumb, sloppiness, and other habits that typically evolve, which for practical reasons are used to circumvent cumbersome security routines. This at a scale, speed, and level of effectiveness previously unseen. Pattern recognition tools, and in particular neural networks, are especially useful in capturing overlooked practices that are forming detectable patterns which corporates are rarely aware of, officially at least. Exploiting these anomalies is often the chosen insertion point in hit-and-run attacks.

- **Anonymity**. The originator, and source, of the attack has often proven hard, even impossible, to identify. Operating under anonymity, or indeed even in disguise, is often a deliberate part of a digital warfare strategy. Its ubiquitous and unpredictable characteristics have changed the way in which war is waged and battles are fought. The anonymous nature of digital warfare is complicating and to some degree even preventing traditional risk mitigation such as pre-emptied deterrence and the threat of retaliation. This anonymity also allows for performing an orchestration of attacks in a hybrid fashion, including in multiple domains and platforms, perhaps with the view of giving the impression of multiple foes attacking in a coordinated manner. The improved artificial intelligence techniques can in particular help to reduce the reliance on the often traceable "command and control" phase of malware, as these are becoming more autonomous, also the establishment of fake social media identities and deepfakes are notable upgrades of the fraudulent aspects of attacks.

- **Opportunistic**. When the preferred strategy is to attack networks and systems, the timing of the intended digital attack is dependent on finding security vulnerabilities that can be exploited, something which can never be guaranteed beforehand. But with the capabilities to systematically and constantly scan for weaknesses, the likelihood for finding opportunities will increase, albeit these might not necessarily be identified at the preferred target, which might trigger opportunistic attacks. However, attacks on brands and reputations are less subject to such considerations and can be targeted in a more pre-timed and deliberate manner.

- **Scalability**. As artificial intelligence algorithms can better analyse patterns and at a wider scale than what previous algorithms have been able to, more potential patterns may be identified highlighting weaknesses to be exploited. And such a pattern-detecting algorithm can be scaled more efficiently if it is designed to operate autonomously, not needing oversight of human handlers on when and how to attack.

Applying the CHAOS acronym on the emerging technical capabilities that artificial intelligence provides means that almost every corporation needs to establish defence capabilities that include the capacity to identify artificial intelligence code that is scanning for patterns in data that it can use as an attack vector. The method to do so is for the defensive framework to deploy artificial intelligence algorithms to seek out and counter any algorithms that operate with an offensive purpose or at a minimum know their base patterns of how the systems and employees normally behave, including what components usually resides there, something which is bound to trigger a digital arms race.

A full-scale digital war, or a hybrid approach with considerable digital input, will, in accordance to Clausewitz's theory, aim to target schwerpunkts as the most efficient (and quickest) means to achieve its objectives. Both an organisation's technological infra-structure as well as its brand can be considered default schwer-punkts. What the characteristics of these highlight is that they are targets of an economic nature, which to a large degree depends on digital technologies, from both the offensive and defensive perspec-tive. And as noted in the CHAOS acronym, the many advantages that digital warfare provides for an attacker will ensure that economic and political objectives are the preferred options rather than, as in the past, seeking to conquer physical possessions of territories, or as in this context the actual takeover of the corporation. The prepa-ration of a digital attack does not require assembling an army of soldiers with an extensive arsenal of armoury and the complicated logistical arrangements that such preparations require, including ensuring that the armed forces actually are motivated enough to fight a war where their lives might be at stake, something which history has shown to often be a major impediment. Quality will precede quantity, and a successful venture is likely if an attacker is able to gather bright minds with an intense interest in IT security, and especially how to circumvent it. Also, an attack can be con-ducted from the safety of one's own premises, with virtually no risk of life and no need to physically having to enter another country. Attribution, as noted, is far from straightforward, and this opaque digital underworld allows the attacker to operate under the guise of ambiguity, which, if paired with a designated psychological warfare operation, means that blame can be directed towards other actors in a "conquer and divide" approach, sowing confusion which will fur-ther the efficiency of such an attack. As Chapter 4 highlighted, the improved functionality of digital weapons through AI-enabled tech-niques, capable of acting autonomously and constantly sniffing out security vulnerabilities, will make the defence arrangements against them increasingly more difficult to maintain. A combatant initiating digital attacks will have two main objectives, either penetrating and targeting the adversary's, or an affiliated third party's, network and systems with a view to perform espionage or sabotage, or target the brand and reputation, seeking temporary or permanent damage through deploying psychological warfare operations mainly on various public social media platforms.

A full-scale, all-encompassing digital attack would likely target a corporate's both major schwerpunkts, namely its brand and its systems. It could, as a standard scenario, unfold in three phases, to a large degree mirroring the strategy applied in conventional warfare.

THE FIRST PHASE: PSYCHOLOGICAL WARFARE AND DIGITAL INSURGENCY

The objective of a psychological warfare operation is to alter the perception of a corporation's image into a negative fashion in the eyes of the general public or the specific target group. Suddenly in social media, and perhaps also mainstream media, articles with negative contents start to appear, which might include both ferocious and subtle attacks seeking to destroy the reputation of the corporation, in at least one aspect. Generally, the critique takes aim at contentious contemporary issues, such as the corporation in question not adhering to environmental standards, disregarding standard equality policies, or being involved in outright criminal acts. This could include fabricated reports of discrimination which can lead to increased public scrutiny with the risk of damaging its brand and reputation. Or a public company might experience significant drop in stock price if fake news using misquoted statements by senior management starts to spread like wildfire on social media. The content can either be altogether manufactured, albeit usually containing small grains of truth which are magnified and distorted far beyond reasonable proportions, or damaging confidential information which has been collated through espionage. By creating social discord, the psychological foundation of the targeted corporation is becoming undermined. The lack of filtering allows for well-crafted fake news to reach social media where it can, depending on purpose, either have a short-term shock effect or a more permanent negative influence corroding the positive image of the brand. Most of such news campaigns will seek to trigger an emotional response and if nothing else establish doubts on whether one can actually trust the targeted corporation. Influencing public opinion through social media channels, even obscure such, will, if cleverly done, often also reverberate into mainstream media, and can be conducted on a relatively small budget. Its effects can be augmented and distributed through automated means, such as orchestrated social media accounts and chatbots creating a perception of popularity and great interest from the general public. The chatbots' assignment is to conjure the algorithms of social networks into believing that the planted articles or posts receive a lot of support by other seemingly real users which creates the perception of a commonly shared opinion that makes it look like there is huge support for an argument, while in fact it is fabricated.

By now and probably not unbeknownst to anyone, the veritable explosion of content and users on the various social media with different perspectives and agendas has made the concept of truth highly fluid and elusive. We have entered an era where lies, half-lies, conspiracies, suspicions, and open secrets have become integrated elements of (social) reality. It is an environment where corporations that pride themselves on maintaining integrity and trust find they are operating in a challenging setting, as there is always a risk of someone questioning them and their motives, and sometimes for sinister reasons. It is an established insight that trust takes a long time to build, years or even decades, but can evaporate in matter of minutes. In such a multidimensional landscape, humans come to operate by rules-of-thumb and generalised assumptions to help them navigate a fragmented world and avoid an overload of information. Obviously, by applying these heuristic shortcuts, mainly through the force of habit, cognitive errors are bound to occur, something which a receptive enemy can capitalise on in designing deceptive campaigns to alter narratives.[1,2]

As the concept of truth is being watered out to the point of becoming a relative term, a certain nihilistic sentiment is bound to become prevalent which means that credibility will be difficult to uphold if attacks are made against the integrity of a brand. An adversary can through a dedicated strategy of spreading doubts on the validity of statements of a certain corporation, over time, bring about an element of distrust which can erode its economic value. And in an atmosphere thriving on gossip, such doubts can take a life of its own, something which makes it increasingly difficult for the attacked company to defend itself, and eventually all its statements will be viewed with at least some suspicion. In that sense, not only is it information that is being weaponised but this ambiguity becomes in itself a weapon. The typical next step is to orchestrate a "fast burning crisis," often in the form of shocking truths. However, whilst it is recognised that negative news especially of a shocking truth nature spreads faster than any other type of news, it still is a hazardous undertaking for the attacker to achieve the desired effect as targeting the intended audience is both complex and fragmented, as they must find the right content, tone, timing, and appropriate platform.[3] Leveraging known inherent human psychological weaknesses is one approach to cunningly lure the targets to adjust their behaviour in accordance with the sought-after effect. One of the most known of these psychological phenomena is the *Thomas Theorem*, which suggests that "if men define situations as real, they are real in their consequences."[4] In effect, it means that if one is able, through psychological operations, to change the interpretation of a situation, the influenced individuals will respond accordingly, even if these beliefs are factually wrong. Hence, by seeking to redefine perceptions, even towards erroneous or false ones, of a situation, one can tilt the probabilities of the recipients taking an action, or if the preferred response is inertia, in one's favour. Artificial intelligence algorithms can test what content works and what does not over and over again on millions of people at high speed, until their targets react as desired.[5] It is likely that artificial intelligence will be used to exploit the weaknesses inherent in human nature at a scale, speed, and level of effectiveness previously unseen. Emerging technologies will allow this loop of iterative refinements to occur almost instantaneously, where the algorithms will be closely aligned with heuristics such as the Thomas Theorem.[6]

In Russian intelligence circles, methods have been developed at least since the 1960s to systematically be able to take advantage of these human psychological patterns. It is referred to as "reflexive control theory" which aspires to manipulate human perceptions of reality.[7] The gist of the theory is to identify the most efficient strategy to transmit information to the intended targets, both in terms of timing and content, to subtly change their underlying motives and the way they make decisions, this by making them believe that there is in their best interest to take a certain action, even if it is not objectively so. The previously described generative adversarial networks which currently are mostly being used to build whimsical deepfakes for fake porn videos and political satire, but the swift improvement of quality are making them harder to distinguish from genuine film clips and they will become an important part of psychological warfare operations. These can be produced almost instantaneously as the iterative comparisons between generator and discriminator neural networks that align it with the authentic material are operating at machine speed with high accuracy. What is equally worrying is that any collated feedback to these deepfakes can serve as input to yet another generative adversarial network, where these are analysed to learn how to better craft manipulative posts as a response, which within quite a short time frame can find the right tone to push its targets to start changing attitudes, preferences, or behaviours in the sought-after direction.[8]

An important part of these campaigns is not to disclose that the designated news and postings are indeed a deliberate deception, so they are generally conducted clandestinely, where the instigators go to great lengths to obscure not only themselves but their motives; from that perspective, psychological warfare is in essence undeclared war. Hence, they must be crafted in such ways that they appropriately reverberate with the intended audience's likes and dislikes in accordance with their moral and psychological inclinations, which are gathered through collating data on psychological profiles, and focus the attention and efforts on the basis this data. By applying such a "filter," it provides the path to a schwerpunkt of an abstract nature.[9]

Beyond the propaganda efforts, this first phase also includes an infiltration into the target's network and systems, which will create the basis for the second phase of attack, where planted malware attempts to take control or sabotage the IT infrastructure or applications. This initiates the ensuing second phase.

THE SECOND PHASE: GREY ZONE WARFARE

When sufficient doubts have been planted on the prospects of moral righteousness or economic viability of the target corporation, and malware have been covertly installed, the second phase may commence. It will mostly operate in a grey zone environment, meaning that the legal consequences might not be all that straightforward. And in such an environment, intent and motivation can be difficult to ascertain, including identifying links to suspected perpetrators, also the modus operandi of the operations might wilfully be obscured or copied in the fashion of known hacker groups to further cover the tracks. This will make digital forensics in the quest to assign responsibilities and gather evidence a challenging, and in some cases an impossible, task. By not knowing the underlying motives and the identity of the attacker, it establishes an atmosphere of uncertainty, in which it becomes difficult for the attacked to reassure that they are actually in charge of what happens, and perhaps more importantly what might happen next. The chaos and disorder this brings with it further undermines the trust in and credibility of the target, depicting them as helpless, not knowing what to expect next or when it will stop, if at all. In accordance with Clausewitz theories, it will be the schwerpunkts that will provide the best entry points in an attack, as they render the opponent most vulnerable. Defenders must continuously evaluate the levels of difficulty of penetrating the security measures, not only surrounding the critical IT resources vis-à-vis lesser defended applications and systems in the periphery, even outsourced such, that still might corrupt overall accessibility and functionality and leave a damaged reputation. Hence, it will require a comprehensive digital due diligence to make sure that any subcontractors and their subcontractors, including cloud system providers and seemingly inconspicuous applications, and so forth, are compliant with security regulations and the expected minimum standards, which should be a pivotal consideration of establishing defence arrangements. Given the expenses such arrangements usually imply, outsourcing or subcontracting negotiations must ascertain and price in the costs for digital security throughout the entire supply chain. The mode of attack as well as its timing will be at the attacker's prerogative, usually choosing to launch first once the malware has been put in place and made operational, initiating psychological warfare undertakings at a time when, for some reason, the target might already be vulnerable. Herewith, operating in the shady grey zone becomes particularly advantageous for the attacker.

THE THIRD PHASE: OPEN WARFARE

The final phase can take a hybrid approach where more conventional means of fighting an (economic) war can facilitate the digital approach, such as threatening with economic or political blackmail. This with a view to finally eradicate the defender's organised resistance. It can include takeover of assets whose values have been temporarily destroyed and corrupted, and hence now can be had on the cheap. But it can also mean death, in other words driving a competitor, or if it is the short seller's target, into bankruptcy and liquidation. Or the attacker might force the target to accept a standard or products being promoted by its affiliates, or seek to dominate its flow of information, in effect deciding under what narrative the targeted company will have to operate under going forward. What, in a sense, will distinguish digital warfare of today and tomorrow versus that of yesterday is that the features of artificial intelligence are in an increasing degree automating activities to the point of them becoming semi-automated or fully automated where they were previously largely manual. They will be able to dynamically generate new malware and change features in themselves to avoid detection.

In particular, there are certain themes where the newer versions of autonomous artificial intelligence will be particularly influential:

- *Aggregation*, where artificial intelligence applications can more succinctly and swiftly collect, collate, fuse, and analyse data on a much vaster scale than previously with a view to identify patterns allowing for the construction of much more precise malware, enabling them a higher degree of probability to circumvent security arrangements in a bespoke manner rather than the current mainly standardised approach
- *Repetition*, where these can provide an ability to generate more consistent and persistent repetitions of tasks and actions than most existing artificial intelligence applications which require human supervision, with the sometimes considerable degree of manual work can currently muster, something which affects the scale and magnitude of digital attacks
- *Deception*, including social engineering operations where machine generated responses and similar appear more humanlike than ever, they can produce the impression of a real human being on the other side and if equipped with privy information, such as collating language samples through natural language processing software and mimic jargon to create a feeling of familiarity, be able to snare targets. This need not only be directed towards humans but other applications and software that operate to gauge whether it is a man or machine on the other side, such as spam or bot filters.

COMBATANTS

Digital combatants can be thought of in six main categories, and interestingly, there are a number of attacks where these have cooperated in ways that have not been commonly seen in conventional warfare; thus there exist considerable blurred boundaries between them. Not only will their motivations differ, albeit at times overlap, but also their capacity, which to a large degree but not exclusively is linked to their allocated budgets. These are:

1 **State sponsored entities**. State-sponsored entities consist of a variety of agencies, digital armed forces or parts of intelligence services, which are sometimes organised as affiliated "private" security firms in which the state holds an influencing stake. These can act as conduits to recruit talented individual hackers or hacker groups to be consulted for particular projects, not always being clear who they ultimately actually are working for. State-sponsored entities are generally the most well funded of the digital combatants. Mostly their operations are focused on psychological warfare to promote a preferred political narrative, influencing foreign governments to adhere to their demands, or trying to create political, social, or ethnic instability in targeted nations. But also espionage, not only focused on military objectives but notably having shown a great interest in illicitly collating economic information and intellectual property which are provided to domestic firms to enhance their competitiveness. To a lesser extent they engage in sabotage, which also can include proxy targets, such as banks and energy companies forming the bedrock of the countries they are attacking; the Russian digital attacks against Estonia and Ukraine are cases in point. In particular China, North Korea, and Russia have been highlighted as proactive states in digital attacks. As they also have access to armed forces, diplomatic and political tools, their digital operations can be part of broader hybrid political/warfare strategies.

2 **Criminal groups**. Their strategies will range from the simplistic distributed denial-of-service (DDoS) attacks and less sophisticated malware to more advanced tools seeking to extract money through extortion and blackmail, where deepfakes are anticipated to play a future important role. Their strategies involve not only attacking networks and systems but can also include campaigns threatening to destroy a corporation's reputation. At the less refined part of the spectra are typically younger, less

experienced individuals who tend to commit crimes with cruder and simpler tools, and subsequently with limited damage. They can usually be identified and brought to justice relatively easily through standard tracking tools. More sophisticated criminal attackers are centred on elaborate financial crimes, sometimes ingenious schemes, and disrupting services. At the top of the criminal pyramid are the most well organised, seeking to ensure untraceability before commencing operations, often targeting high-profile corporations or government organisations by using state-of-the-art digital weapons and tools, and at times these criminal ventures are state-sponsored operations.

3 **Hackers**. These often constitute the groups with the most advanced and ingenious technical skills and is the category where a raft of new digital weapons is being designed and developed. They are defined by a certain bravado which includes trying to break security arrangement considered unbreakable for the sake of it, this to achieve a legendary heroic status in their community's folklore. Typically, they seek the technical challenge to hack into systems, or expose organisations they regard as "evil" as the ulterior motives. The more dubious individuals or groups of this category can freelance for state-sponsored entities or criminal groups.

4 **Hacktivists**. This is the most ideologically coloured category, which include human right activists, libertarians, environmentalists, and extends to political and religious extremists across the left-right range. Their main objective is to attack what they view as opponents or enemies against their own agendas. The digital attacks can be an integrated part of wider-scale terrorist attacks, attempting to destroy both physical and digital targets, and simultaneously promote their cause.

5 **Corporations**. This category in particular refers to private security firms, public relation agencies, and advertising or media outlets focused on the different parts of a digital warfare operation, typically acting as mercenaries on behalf of states or its affiliates but unlike criminal groups remaining on the right side of the

law. However, these kinds of corporations domiciled in authoritarian countries, notably China and Russia, have shown a history of engaging in extensive hacking with a view of stealing intellectual property and facilitating state agencies as required. They also engage in influencing campaigns, extending to psychological warfare, where they seek to undermine competitors, sometime by sponsoring hacktivists to act as useful idiots to ensure they keep an arms-length distance to activities viewed as shady.

6   **Individuals.** Can either be disgruntled ex-employees that take whistle-blowing to another level, exposing perceived corporate injustices through publicising confidential information or attempting to sell it to the highest bidder, or exceptionally tech-savvy individuals seeking income, with some of them taking a digital-guns-for-hire approach, having in essence become mercenaries that the more resource-strong combatants come to employ.

A full-scale digital attack will assign different roles and responsibilities, not always formally delineated and clearly defined but usually arranged as follows:

- **Initiator**, who can also be the sponsor of the attack, or the individual assigned by the sponsor whose main responsibility is to plan, coordinate, control, and manage the attack
- **Specialists**, recruited to execute various key tasks of the attack, mainly of a technical nature but can also include linguists and psychologists
- **Sources**, can be insiders of the targeted corporation that get financially compensated to leak sensitive information about security installations, or confidential information that can influence the economic value of the company if made public in a sensational context
- **Transmitters and channels**, which refine and calibrate raw data from the sources, adapting them for public consumption, which are then released on various social media platforms, ideally in such a context where they immediately will reach the intended audience

- **Intermediaries**, employed to facilitate the distribution of the information

These resources can operate in separate teams, unbeknownst to each other, making attribution and tracking the initiator and sponsor a difficult undertaking. However, as a rule the more complex these operations are, the more likely they have a state involvement acting in a sponsor capacity (Figure 5.1).

GUIDELINES ON HOW TO ORGANISE A DIGITAL DEFENCE

Corporations must, as this book highlights, approach the risk for digital attacks from a suite of different potential combatants with a variety of motives and techniques and also now need to incorporate an additional perspective to the traditional considerations of cyber security, namely:

- There needs to be a requirement to ascertain and assess the various traces of data patterns they are leaving in the digital space and thoroughly understand how these might constitute battle grounds, and therefore ensure that adequate resources are made available so they can be mitigated or as far as possible eliminated.
- There needs to be an appreciation, that so far mostly failed to be acknowledged, of the emerging holistic approach to digital warfare that combatants are organising their strategies by, in essence a blitzkrieg in nature and duration which will include many types of weapons, of which some might not only be of a digital construct. By understanding these strategies, corporations are better equipped to establish what phase a potential attack might be in, and what to expect thereafter. Thus, realising the weaknesses as a consequence of having a digital presence, a cost of doing business of sorts, they will be better equipped to offset any attacks which for most must be viewed as the inevitable.

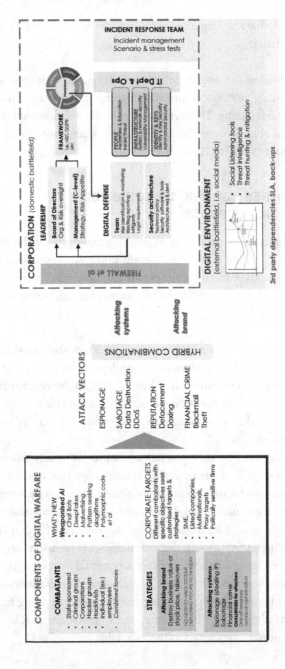

Figure 5.1 An overview of the strategic options available to combatants engaging in digital warfare.

These perspectives should form the basis for the arrangements of a viable defence framework. Digital warfare has gone beyond being merely attacks against technologies, whether hardware and software, and there is a social dimension with all data traces that are increasingly being used as an insertion point for attacks. Thus, by promoting an understanding of the digital patterns, and realising that these patterns are not static but fluid and dynamic in character, constantly changing over time, as new products and services, distribution channels, and employees and partners emerge, capturing and ringfencing them is a key mitigant in dealing with digital attacks.

THE DIGITAL DEFENCE FRAMEWORK

A digital defence framework needs to start with an understanding of the anatomy of digital attacks, broken down into the various classes that represent established strategies. Through ascertaining and mapping ongoing hostile activities against these, a properly organised digital defence stands the best chance to reduce, or if possible completely eradicate the full impact of such attacks (Figure 5.2).

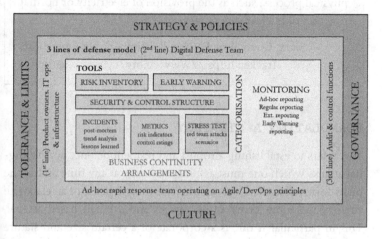

Figure 5.2   A graphical depiction of the digital defence framework.

FACT SHEET: CLASSIFYING DIGITAL ATTACKS

Data Destruction. The use of malicious software to destroy data on a computer or to render a computer inoperable.

Defacement. The unauthorized act of changing the appearance of a website or social media account.

Distributed Denial of Service. The intentional paralyzing of a computer network by flooding it with data sent simultaneously from many individual computers.

Doxing. The act of searching and publishing private or identifying information about an individual or group on the internet, typically with malicious intent.

Espionage. The act of obtaining confidential information without the information holder's consent.

Financial Theft. The theft of assets, such as cryptocurrencies or cash, for financial gain.

Sabotage. The use of malware that causes a disruption to a physical process, such as the provision of electricity or normal function of nuclear centrifuges.

Source: Council on Foreign Relations. Cyber Operations Tracker. https://www.cfr.org/cyber-operations/.

FORMULATING A STRATEGY

This refers to establishing a robust and resilient defence against digital attacks which one must assume can occur at any time and in the many forms described and can often be a single phase of an elaborate strategy including many attack vectors and a broad based arsenal. This in particular if one is a corporate of a certain size and stature that can be expect to at some point be attacked out of a variety of motives from a diverse variety of combatants. A multitiered defence framework can ensure that layers of checks and balances are able to act in a coordinated manner. Hence, it should embrace a holistic perspective, embedded in an overarching culture concerned with the threats and risks the corporation might be exposed to. This is at the metalevel articulated through a "no surprise" culture where a hierarchy of monitoring and visualising of risks across the corporation with assigned roles and responsibilities to promptly address and escalate any emerging incidents becomes the guiding principle on which a digital defence is established.

The primary document that governs and formalises the appropriate culture needs to be a strategy document ratified by both the senior management and board of directors to signify its importance and equal standing of other guiding documents that highlights the fundamental principles of the corporation. The objective of the strategy should be to formalise and communicate the organisation's approach to defending itself against digital attacks, including its methods to the identification, assessment, management, measuring, monitoring, and reporting of all potential risks relating to digital warfare it might be exposed to now and in the future. A strategy document outlining the digital defence should at a minimum include the following objectives:

- Contribute towards the generation of client and shareholder value, enhanced customer value and service, the attainment of strategic and business objectives, and protection of the corporations' assets, including the wellbeing of its employees and the minimisation of criminal endeavours across businesses and regions.
- Assist the board of directors and senior management to articulate and to cascade the overall risk tolerance and strategies in the management of a digital defence.
- Recommend policies and guidelines to control and strengthen the corporation's digital defence
- Establish a culture of awareness and ownership through communication and education of the risk of digital attacks at all relevant

levels of the corporation, supported at both the business unit level and the support unit functions endorsed by senior management and, if any, a committee empowered with executive powers to conduct reviews and request enhancements

- Clarify the roles, responsibilities, and accountabilities across the whole business for the identification, assessment, management, measurement, monitoring, and reporting of all risks pertaining to digital warfare, this through the establishment of a three lines of defence model.

- Guide the establishment and maintenance of a robust and consistent approach for the identification and assessment of digital attack incidents throughout the corporation.

- Assist senior management throughout the corporation to identify, assess, manage, monitor, and report effectively the risks of digital attacks to which their respective businesses may be exposed via a systematic process of ongoing control and risk (self-)assessments and stress testing of security arrangements, such as red team testing.

- Guide the establishment on a consistent process to regularly monitor the status of its digital defence framework and risk of being exposed to digital attacks by gathering and analysing a raft of data, including external intelligence and regularly report, or in the situation of emergency ad hoc reporting, of the findings to senior management and the board of directors.

- Advise on the development of a consistent approach to reporting of digital exposures viable for attacks via appropriate data gathering and external intelligence and associated escalation procedures to be applied across the corporation, allowing senior management, committees and the board of directors to review and challenge pertinent issues and assess business unit performance in this area versus risk tolerances and limits.

- Establish a process that requires all new products, communication and distribution channels, mergers and acquisitions, disposals, processes, systems, and services are subject to an adequate assessment and due diligence prior to commencement.

- Support the effective, comprehensive, independent, and ongoing challenge to be provided by the internal audit function and other control units in relation to the appropriateness and adequacy of existing security arrangements and controls throughout the corporation.

A WEB OF POLICIES

As the types of digital attacks come in different forms, and even if a corporation has a dedicated digital defence unit, some of the potential digital risk exposures will be the main responsibilities of other functions. That is depending on jurisdiction and industry, external regulations and standards that either are mandatory, or of such stature that one is expected to adhere to these. The practical implementation of the guiding principles in the strategy document are outlined in a hierarchy of policy documents, some crafted for the digital defence function, whereas others are in parts captured through other functions' roles and responsibilities. The policies should be mapped out and linked so that any potential entanglement of policies can be comprehended and adjusted to avoid control gaps that could arise between and within functions. The policies that should be considered would typically include the following.

- A policy outlining the roles and responsibilities of the digital defence team
- **Board of directors operating polices**
  - board expectations
  - hierarchical and organisational structure
  - strategic and business development
  - reputation, public relations, and brand management
  - control environment and audit responsibilities
- **Code of business conduct and ethics policy**
- **New product, business and services approval policy**
- **Anti-money laundering policy and customer relations policy**
  - know your customer policy
  - service standards

- customer and relationship management
- data protection, i.e. GDPR
- **Human resource policies**
  - workplace and health and safety
  - recruitment
  - employment practices, including social media conduct
  - personal share dealing and investments
  - training and education
  - performance appraisal
- **Regulatory, legal and compliance policy**
  - corporate actions and events
  - litigation and legal risks
  - powers of attorney and signing authorities
  - disclosure ("whistle-blowing")
- **Fraud prevention policy**
- **Outsourcing and vendor control policy**
- **Business continuity policy**
- **Risk tolerance policy statement**

GOVERNANCE STRUCTURE

A widely recognised governance model, especially in the financial services, to ensure an efficient handling of a widespread range of risks, including such relating to the many dimensions of technology is the three lines of defence model (Figure 5.3). It is designed on the principle that roles and responsibilities for managing risks needs to be clearly defined as it forms the foundation for a systematic method of identifying and reviewing risks, in this context adjusted to fit the requirements of a digital defence structure.

- **The first line of defence**. The board of directors sets the acceptable tolerance for digital risks, approves the strategy for the digital defence function and is responsible for the security arrangements and associated internal controls. It approves appropriate policies on these and seeks regular assurance, supported by the

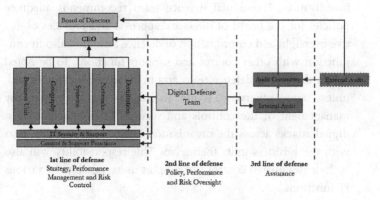

Figure 5.3 The three lines of defence governance model.

internal audit, or if applicable audit committee, that enables it to satisfy itself that the security is functioning effectively, and that it is managing the risk for digital attacks in the manner that it has approved. The chief executive officer, supported by senior management, has overall responsibility for the digital risks facing the organisation and is supported in the management of these by the digital defence team, business unit, and support unit heads. The chief executive officer reports regularly to the board of directors on the management of digital risk across the organisation. Management and staff within each business unit have the primary responsibility for managing the risk for being exposed to digital attacks. They must take personal ownership for the identification, assessment, management, monitoring, and reporting of any risks arising within their respective areas of responsibility.

- **The second line of defence** is comprised of the digital defence team. They provide operational and technical support and advice to both senior management and business unit level management. Any assistance in the identification, assessment, management, measurement, monitoring, and reporting of the risk of digital attacks is primarily by way of oversight and as required investigation. The digital defence team recommends adequate policies for the board of directors' approval and provides objective oversight and co-ordination of defence activities, also in conjunction with other control and support functions. To be noted is that the digital defence team acts in an advisory capacity and, unless stated otherwise, is not accountable for the day-to-day management of the controls and security arrangement against digital attacks across the organisation as this responsibility rests with the business units themselves. This responsibility will also include designated control and support units, notably the various IT functions.

- **The third line of defence** provides independent objective assurance on the effectiveness of the digital defence across the entire organisation. This is provided to the board of directors through the internal audit function and, if established, the board audit committee, which are supported by the external auditor who reports directly to the shareholders.

For some industries, notably banking and insurance, a risk management function has since long been an integrated part of the organisation, and by requirements from financial regulators. Its roles and responsibilities include the management of financial risks, which consists of mainly credit and market risk, and operational risks, including technology risks and fraud risks, which largely would overlap with some of the categories that constitutes digital attacks, except attacks on brand and reputation. The three lines of defence governance model was developed with a risk management function in mind, hence if such a model already exists within the organisation, a digital defence team can be embedded and integrated into it with expanded responsibilities and broadened skillsets, including a proactive approach of gathering intelligence externally and working with industry groups and law enforcement to mitigate the risk of digital attacks. An already existing risk management function would also need an in-depth expertise in artificial intelligence. However, for corporations outside the financial industry, a risk management unit does often not exist and a digital defence team needs to find its place between the business units, IT functions, and control units, such as internal audit. What are then the roles and responsibilities of the digital defence team?

As the three lines of defence model states, its main function is advisory, unless stated otherwise. Its main responsibilities include that of providing tools to identify, monitor, measure, and report all relevant information pertaining to the risks of digital attacks and conduct ad hoc investigations and coordinate the arrangement of temporary measure to divert ongoing attacks. The digital defence team acts as the centre of excellence on all aspects of digital warfare in the organisation. Its key role is to ensure the effective and timely completion of tasks related to the identification and remedy of significant digital risks. In case of any regulatory contacts and reporting requirements relating to digital warfare, the team acts as the liaison point. Some of the key responsibilities include:

- Provide and guide business units with stress tests, red team tests, and scenarios on existing security arrangements and feedback on results, and as required provide advice on necessary improvements.
- Generate guidelines on tolerance/limit levels of acceptable digital risks.
- Help assess the effectiveness of alternative risk mitigation strategies.
- Provide assistance in training and education in the area of digital warfare.
- Provide regular and ad hoc reporting and management information regarding the risk of digital attacks.
- Collate and monitor appropriate indicators, incident information, status on controls, and other appropriate digital risk tracking metrics.
- Aggregate data and maintain the digital risk inventory.
- Analyse and validate digital risk data.
- Provide senior management and the board of directors with regular reporting on digital risks and the results of specific investigations.

- Ensure continued research and implementation of adequate tools and techniques to strengthen the digital defence.
- Advise on the digital warfare perspectives of policies and major business and strategy changes.
- Help identify digital risks inherent to new products and business lines.
- Act as the key point for the gathering of external intelligence relating to the various aspects of digital warfare.
- Coordinate as required with external parties, including regulators, law enforcement, and industry groups working proactively to address the risks of digital attacks. This could include information sharing and resource and tool allocation.
- In the case of ongoing attacks, swiftly establish an ad hoc response team under the direct leadership of the digital defence team, being empowered to call in the resources deemed required to on the go develop countermeasures and temporary security arrangements to prevent the escalation of an attack, engage in damage limitation or outright termination of an ongoing threat.

To facilitate the work of the digital defence team, each business unit and control and support function appoint a contact person on all matters relating to digital attacks. As highlighted, some of the control and security arrangements relating to digital risks will be maintained under other related policies and are part of regulatory legislation and scrutiny. An overview and coordination of these policies and requirements to ensure no control gaps might arise are administered by the digital defence team.

THE TOOLBOX OF THE DIGITAL DEFENCE TEAM

For a digital defence to function efficiently, the inclusion of tools should follow an iterative framework where digital exposures prone to attacks are identified, assessed, controlled, and reported in a disciplined and transparent manner in accordance to seeking resolution as required and ongoing monitoring. The upholding of a digital

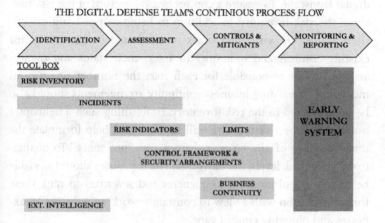

THE DIGITAL DEFENSE TEAM'S CONTINUOUS PROCESS FLOW

Figure 5.4 The three lines of defence governance model.

defence is thus a continuous process, in which overlapping activities are inscribed in cycles of different length depending on their immediate need and the nature of the activity. The key processes, to which appropriate tools are assigned, include (Figure 5.4):

- identification
- assessment
- controls/mitigants
- monitoring and reporting

THE RISK INVENTORY

Through the creation of a risk inventory which is maintained and continuously upgraded by the digital defence team, which can be organised through a classification system that defines digital attacks, a continuous overview of what risks the corporation is exposed to can be articulated. The risks which may be identified through the review of previous incidents, security vulnerabilities as highlighted through stress tests, investigations and audit reports, and through external intelligence will facilitate the pinpointing of risks in the digital landscape. To ensure a comprehensive picture of the risk universe, the risk inventory, in addition to being mapped and categorised against known digital attack types, should be pinned against existing controls and indicators to assess their status and owners assigned to be responsible for each risk, the number of previous incidents and existing business continuity arrangements should also be incorporated in the risk inventory. Establishing such a helicopter oversight of the risk universe will facilitate and help formulate the understanding of any broader themes and "hot spots." To qualitatively gauge risk levels, the individual risk exposures should as viable be linked to estimates on frequencies and severities to rank these for prioritisation with a view to constantly work on reducing weaknesses and plugging control gaps.

DIGITAL ATTACK INCIDENTS

By collating and disseminating previous incidents of digital attacks, a corporate memory providing a source of "lessons learned" and trend analysis that can give valuable insights of the type of attacks, strategies, malware, if possible type of combatants, and digital battlefield that have previously occurred can be established. This, however, requires an in-depth post-mortem examination of each incident following a standardised investigation routine and template. This process should operate with the view of minimising the future risk of similar incidents. The repository where the incidents are stored should allow for multi-dimensional analysis, as it must be designed to house both information of quantitative as well as qualitative nature regarding the financial losses by category, causal factor(s), business unit, process affected, date, etc. as per reporting rules. These should be categorised and collated to allow the study of recurring trends and patterns. An important part of the post-mortem is to ascertain whether there is a bigger picture, such as does it appear that an individual attack is part of something bigger? Are we the only organisation being attacked? Could this be a proxy attack? As part of this analysis it is important to identify the perpetrators and assign attribution which might have to be conducted through the cooperation with national and international law enforcements, also to ensure that legal consequences and potential retribution can be administered. The post-mortem also needs to include a practical "lessons learned" phase covering:

- established entry point and type of malware
- categorisation of the incident
- establish how much data was compromised or stolen
- identify any customers or third parties that have been affected
- perform a comprehensive security review to ensure that the virus still is not lurking in the network or systems
- update security policies to prevent a similar attack from taking place in the future
- for attacks on brand occurring on social media, an alternate set of information needs to be gathered and analysed

RISK INDICATORS

Indicators are designed to measure the risks identified and incorporated in the risk inventory. As such they provide information relating to specific items within certain processes. These items can help predict specific risks. They could indicate that there are problems in a given process that could lead to losses should a digital attack occur. Risk indicators should, as far as possible, be identified in all major processes to ensure a continuous monitoring of the digital environment. Subsequently, adequate management information should be developed to report on the status of these risk indicators, allowing management to introduce measures as required that takes aim at mitigating any control gaps or risks uncovered, thereby avoiding or limiting potential losses. By continuously tracking indicators, levels and emerging trends of risks being on the rise can be unravelled and acted upon. Thus, the construction of a risk indicator must follow one main design principle:

> To capture and correctly reflect the actual level of a risk related to digital attacks.

To ensure that the entire population in the risk inventory is linked to some type of quantitative tracking metrics, a mapping exercise, which can be part of risk and control (self-)assessment, is conducted and aims to pinpoint risk indicators to all identified risk exposures and controls. The way an individual risk indicator is analysed and designed needs to be set in a formulised context (this is normally done on an indicator-by-indicator basis):

- **Single versus aggregate level**. Does it make sense to study and monitor a particular risk indicator in isolation or should the analysis be done in conjunction with other risk indicators?
- **Trends over time**. To better understand the evolvement of digital risk exposures, analysing trends over time can prove very powerful. However, if a certain process has been materially redesigned, systems upgraded or a firewall altered, historical data will be of limited value and hence assessments need to be continuously conducted to evaluate the relevance of historical data for each risk indicator.
- **Frequency of reporting**. How often can an individual risk indicator meaningfully be updated and is that frequent enough for an adequate analysis and management of the associated risk exposure? Can real time monitoring be applied for the full population?
- **Optimising the measurement unit**. Which measurement unit provides the optimal informative value for analysis? Another key question is whether one should focus on absolute or relative values when analysing risk indicators.
- **Types of breakdown**. Normally a risk indicator can be broken down into many different formats. It can be measured by organisational unit, per client, product, system, geographical area, etc. Deciding which breakdown provides the most meaningful information can only be done on a case-by-case basis through granular examination.
- **Frequency versus severity**. Is the risk indicator trying to capture the occurrence of events or the level of actual/potential impact?

Important to note is that the purpose of a digital defence is not to completely eliminate the risk for digital attacks, in parts due to cost reasons but also because the types of digital attacks are constantly evolving and previously unknown types might emerge for which there is no current defence, but to within all reasonable means ensure that the risk for digital attacks are minimised, so that it remains within tolerable boundaries. These boundaries can and should be formalised through the establishment of risk tolerances, in part as a means of benchmarking, which will vary by type of risk and the business unit in which the risk is being assessed or experienced. Subsequently, risk tolerances express how much risk, or the acceptance of certain levels of security vulnerabilities, the organisation is willing to take, and the tolerance can be articulated in both quantitative and qualitative expressions. The tolerance for risk should ideally be quantified in a consistent, realistic, and measurable term to support the rankings of risks not only on a firm-wide level but also for individual business lines and geographies. In addition, tolerance levels can be set for different types of clients, platforms, networks, products, and services to clearly distinguish and ascertain where risk hot spots may lie. Where practically possible, the digital defence team should attempt to conduct quantitative risk analysis to support the setting of tolerance levels, which preferably, albeit not always easy, should be done in monetary terms. The monetary level of risk tolerance deemed acceptable should be aligned with profit targets to get an appropriate understanding of the relationship between risk and return. To facilitate the management of tolerance levels, systems and controls are established to ensure that these are adhered to. In setting risk tolerances, the following guidelines should be considered:

- The board of directors may express its risk tolerance as a single monetary amount that it is willing to risk in pursuit of the corporation's profit target. At a lower level, risk tolerance is as likely to be expressed in non-financial terms as it is in financial terms.
- Risk tolerance must be linked to the overall strategy and objectives of the firm. Risk indicators, the assessment of control and security arrangements and incidents are often used to manage key digital risks and will support the monitoring of tolerance levels. These

metrics will together with documented statements of tolerance levels assist to establish and communicate a culture of risk awareness and consciousness throughout the organisation.

Articulating, setting, and calibrating risk tolerance has implications not only for the digital defence functional model but also for the following elements:

- governance
- managerial policies and processes
- organisational structure
- management information and performance reporting
- training and education
- external reporting

MICROMANAGE THE ORGANISATION THROUGH THE USE OF LIMITS

Tolerances and limits are largely synonymous but are applied on different levels of the organisation, and tolerances normally constitute aggregations of related limits. Basically, tolerances are applied on the firm-wide perspective for separate digital risk types and/or business lines and should be aligned with the corresponding profit estimates. The tolerance levels need, subsequently, as far as possible to be expressed in monetary amounts that the board of directors are willing to risk. However, from the business line perspective, tolerance levels can appear too abstract, so to tie tolerances to more pragmatic and practical targets, limits are introduced. Limits are normally linked to individual risk or controls and are as part of the day-to-day management of the business. The tolerance levels, hence, are cascaded throughout the corporation through limits, which will vary by risk and business line. The limits help service as the board of directors' instrument to communicate the quantitative levels of strategies and objectives as well as a measurable manifest of a culture of risk awareness and consciousness (Figure 5.5).

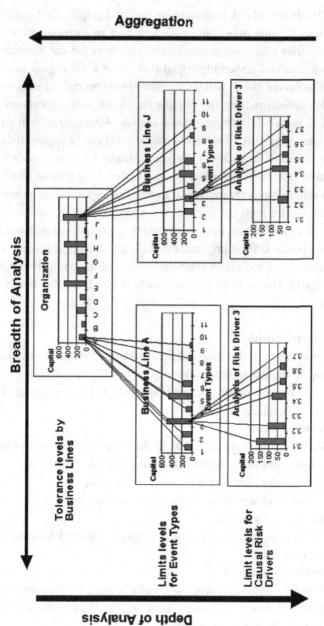

Figure 5.5 Tolerances are cascaded down to limits that relate to individual risk causes for specific risk types and events of digital attacks. Ideally both tolerance and limit levels should be assigned monetary values.

As the trends of risk indicators are depicted graphically, the identification of rising trends, normally equating an increased value of a time series indicating a heightened risk level for the associated exposure, carries a warning signal that the risk for digital attacks might be on the rise. It will be necessary to set up criteria to extract the risk indicators from the population of risk indicators showing warning signals for effective trend analysis. A single uniform rule (e.g. consecutive three data points rising trend) can be applied if data is not sufficient to make an adequate analysis of what constitutes increased risk. There are a few general design principles to observe when setting limits for individual digital risk exposures, manifested and tracked through risk indicators but the calibration can only be done on a case-by-case basis as a number of considerations need to be incorporated. Most importantly, the limits are set in accordance with the related high-level tolerance levels and in conjunction with other limits. Hence, there are three main methods for the design of limits:

1) **Dollar-at-Risk**

   An estimate of the potential financial impact of the items making up the risk indicator value,

   However, a dollar-at-risk amount may not be appropriate for each risk indicator.

2) **Benchmarking**

   The benchmark should be set at the level that the business line believes and aligns with the tolerance for risk,

   Starts to indicate an issue with the process,

   The level at which business lines management are uncomfortable maintaining,

   The level at which senior management should be aware of the concern.

3) **Mechanistic limits**

   Applying statistical rules, such as limit breach whenever a risk indicator value goes above a set range, outside a standard deviation, or above a moving average.

Normally a combination of mechanistic limits and benchmarking are introduced when pure "dollar" levels are not possible to set. To ensure that limits are well integrated into day-to-day management, a number of decisions around the infrastructure need to be made:

- How should any existing supporting IT infrastructure/systems look like?
- Have there been appropriate documentation of tolerance/limit management procedures?
- How are limits embedded into monitoring and reporting?
- How is the limit monitoring best structured? (by whom, how often, reports on limit status, limit exceptions)
- How are treatment of escalation breaches regarding existing preventive action plans, responsibilities, communication lines, materiality, experience, and background to violations adhered to? As limit breaches occur, ensuring that this warning signal is acted upon through issuing escalatory procedures, which will differ depending on the nature of the particular operational risk exposure, is pivotal. Business Continuity Planning and other mitigatory arrangements, which sometimes can be limited to just increasing the awareness of certain issues to reduce the risk of an operational risk loss reducing the levels of loss, need to be linked to each limit setting. After the limits and tolerances are rolled out and implemented as part of the business practice, evaluating their effectiveness will be an ongoing exercise.

Also, as part of monitoring and reporting, the number of limit breaches should be tracked over time to provide trends for further analysis and highlight areas where risk exposures are not contained within tolerable limits. The testing of applied limits versus actual risk indicators and how well they actually relate to ensure that the risks remain within tolerable boundaries is critical to establish credibility of the digital defence framework (Figure 5.6).

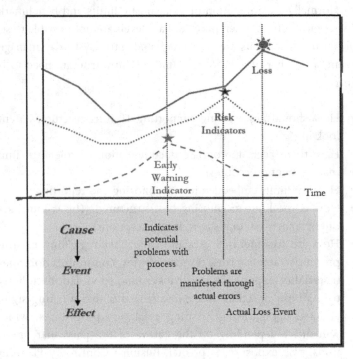

Figure 5.6 By delineating and identifying indicators providing early warnings versus risk indicators highlighting an actual increase in risk levels and subsequent losses, a thorough understanding of how a digital attack unfolds can be gained.

Limits will play a key role in the establishment of an Early Warning System. The objective of an early warning system is to prevent or at least reduce the levels of losses relating to digital attacks, through the identification of predictive indicators and patterns, and linking them to preventive actions.

As early warning signals aim to highlight changes in the digital environment and the effectiveness of the organisation's controls and security framework, it can provide an opportunity to intervene early and avert problems before they become a source of financial loss or damage to the corporation's brand. By continuously collating intelligence to stay abreast of developments in the digital warfare sphere, including new types of malware and tactics deployed, the digital defence team can, based on these insights, stress-test existing controls and defence mechanisms to identify potential vulnerabilities by running war-gaming exercises to educate the employees to improve their handling and skills to address a variety of plausible attacks. Known attacker strategies can be structured along the lines of the CHAOS acronym or similar as a method to better understand how they might unfold should they initiate. Hence, an early warning signal would typically either be a piece of important external intelligence or be the breach of a limit, which indicates that the level of risk for a digital attack has increased and the likelihood of a loss occurring is on the rise. This would merit some type of action, firstly the issuance of an ad hoc report to designated recipients and potentially an investigation of the causes behind the limit breach or the launch of an action plan to reduce the risk of an impending digital attack. These ad hoc early warning reports will augment the regular reporting prepared for different audiences aimed at providing an accurate view of the current status of the risk for digital attacks and the quality of the digital defence.

THE BACKBONE OF DIGITAL DEFENCE: CONTROL AND SECURITY INFRASTRUCTURE

The control and security infrastructure spanning from firewalls and software identifying malware and viruses forms the backbone of digital defence; however, often these are installed and maintained in a fragmented manner, involuntarily leaving potential gaps that a hacker that has conducted meticulous reconnaissance can exploit. However, a study of publicised past failures due to insufficiencies with efficiently mitigating and eliminating digital risks is typically more mundane than the ability of cleverly designed malware managing to circumvent firewalls and similar. The lack of a comprehensive framework clearly outlining roles and responsibilities and action and recovery plans should a digital attack occur typically represents the majority of security failures. An efficient digital defence rests on a few principles:

- the aforementioned three lines of defence framework
- an overarching dual control mechanism, or the "four-eyes principle," to avoid situations where critical or high-risk process or system are effected by a single member of staff only. From a digital defence perspective, business processes that involve sensitive data (static data for customers, contract data and payment data) should be subject to dual control. Whether or not sensitive data is involved should be assessed during the risk classification of the various processes. For high-risk processes, dual control must be obligatory.

The responsibility of assessing the quality of controls, regardless of the actual format they take, should be arranged hierarchically in four levels:

- individual level
- management control
- assessments carried out by specialist units such as Internal Audit or a Corporate Security Department
- assessments carried out by external parties (External Auditors and Supervisory Authorities)

Across these levels, the digital defence team provides advice as required or can, on its own initiative, take action by being responsible for gathering a response team to establish ad hoc security arrangements as deemed necessary with a view to immediately terminate the threat.

CONTROL AT AN INDIVIDUAL LEVEL

To manage risks, staff − regardless of their positions − must view themselves as custodians of risk. Within this context, the digital defence culture and awareness of possible risks play an essential role.

The quality of control at an individual level can be influenced by the following:

- taking preventative measures, including
  - clearly defined decision-making processes for hiring, retaining, and releasing staff, including competence models and assessments based on performance agreements
  - careful selection, appointment, promotion, and training of staff
- optimal communication of policy, culture, applicable values, and, depending on the strategy, objectives and targets
- training, aimed at increased risk awareness
- ensuring that possible repressive measures, such as sanctioning of undesired conduct by staff, are clearly defined and implemented when necessary
- exemplary conduct on the part of (senior) management

MANAGEMENT CONTROL

Given the size of the organisation and the specialised knowledge that is frequently required, management has to delegate tasks and levels of authority. Management will, nevertheless, remain responsible for the tasks it has delegated. For this reason, management must build risk control measures into the business processes and systems. As the party responsible for products and processes, it falls to line-management to create the conditions that safeguard the integrity of products, services, and processes (for example, duty segregation, dual control, system access security). Adequate management information is of pivotal importance in this respect. Supervising the structure of these controls and monitoring their correct functioning is primarily a line-management responsibility. Employees – at all levels – may be discharged of the responsibility to perform tasks delegated to them and have an obligation to account for their actions. This also applies to managing digital risks. This form of delegation, accountability, and control is sometimes referred to as "control via the line" or simply "management control."

ASSESSMENTS BY SPECIALISED UNITS

Because of the size and complexity of the organisation and the specialised knowledge sometimes required, it may be more efficient and effective for (senior) managers not to execute their risk control tasks personally. In such situations, risk control tasks are delegated to specialist functions. The purpose of these specialist functions is to provide (senior) management with an independent expert opinion on risk management within a specific part of the organisation or a given process. Specialised functions may focus on specific types of risks or on specific organisational units. However, the responsibilities of senior and line management cannot be transferred to these specialist functions.

BUSINESS CONTINUITY ARRANGEMENTS: THE IMPORTANCE OF AN AD HOC RESPONSE TEAM

Once an incident has occurred, it is pivotal to have a team and processes in place to swiftly deal with the incident, firstly to put it to a halt and making sure that the business can continue to operate. A key component of a digital defence is to empower a team to handle security incidents until the threat has been neutralised and systems and processes are again fully operational. This should include establishing resources that are able to restore functionality on-the-go and develop preventive arrangements to close the security vulnerability, typically operating on Agile or DevOps methods. But resilience needs to be enabled already at onset, meaning that critical corporate functions must be able to operate under duress; this capacity can be ascertained through stress tests and will include ensuring that backups of data, applications, and even semi-manual operational routines exist if standard routines and data flows have been sabotaged or rendered useless by malware. It also means having employees able to handle these if the ordinary staff for some reason have been put out of play.

ASSESSING CONTROLS

To validate the effectiveness of the control and security infrastructure, they need to be examined for how well they have been designed to prevent the designated digital risk exposures. Stress testing, such as Red Team testing and penetration tests are preferred, albeit resource-demanding, methods that tend to expose control gaps and vulnerabilities. Reviews of risk indicators and historical incidents of digital attacks are other methods of assessing controls. As new types of attacks and other digital risks become acknowledged, the existing control infrastructure needs to be validated on whether it has the capability of preventing attacks of this nature, which can be supplemented by self-appraisal such as a control and risk self-assessment. These are conducted by staff and management (supported by a facilitator) of the organisational unit being assessed, under the supervision of the digital defence team and should be a continuous effort. To complement these, the internal audit unit as part of its remit conducts audits of the various processes. These audits culminate in an audit report (containing all important audit findings and recommendations) and an audit rating (indicating the severity of the findings). The audit reports provides management with important information; it gives them an independent view of the digital defence efforts within the organisation. However, the acceptance of certain digital risks, if entering new markets, products, or platforms, must be gauged against profit projections. Hence, an evaluation of the risk–reward relationship to find the most cost-effective one should accompany a control assessment, providing the following options:

- Eliminate the risk issue by eliminating the function/process along which it lies.
- Reduce the risk by strengthening/building mitigants (including education and training).
- Reduce the risk by insuring it, if possible.
- Keep the risk but re-price the commercial service of which it is a part.

- Accept the risk as manageable and tolerable and establish tolerance and limits accordingly.
- In some cases, decide to increase digital risk exposures, such as establishing new markets and products.

FIGHTING MACHINES WITH MACHINES

The access to new technology should obviously not only be the privilege of culprits but must be an integral part of digital defence as well. Artificial intelligence applications must therefore also play a major role in a defence strategy. These can be deployed to detect seemingly suspicious patterns that might indicate signs of infiltration, highlighting false social profiles, emails containing malwares and so on. Identifying and assessing anomalies will be a key assignment for machine learning tools and this can be made an automated task, replacing manual reviews to an increasing degree. It will dawn on digital defenders that nipping an attack in the bud will be the best approach to survive an attack, and investments in early warning signals and reconnaissance tools detecting any signs of an impending attack will be critical. Obviously, these will always indicate quite a few false positives, requiring manual review and an ongoing calibration of these tools will be part of the screening process.

One can observe an accentuating trend highlighted as an already fierce race between attackers and defenders, which only a few years ago was fairly straightforward; malware could be identified by certain lines of code and coding patterns by an antivirus program that could recognise them as potential threats. To counteract this, malware developers started to create polymorphic code that is able to re-program itself, and thus not permanently having a specific set of code or code pattern but through dynamic features allowed for these to be altered. As a simple example, it would mean that an antivirus software might be looking for a file called "thevirus. exe", but the virus developers realised they could get around this particular security check by randomising the file name to "somethingrandom123.exe". However, the level of sophistication has progressed considerably, more recent antivirus software would look for specific code blocks or patterns belonging to known virus characteristics, so merely renaming a file would not be enough to avoid detection. This in turn has led hackers to create malware that include junk code, or code that rewrites itself, so the pattern changes to avoid detectable patterns. To counter this polymorphism coding, the security community have had to turn to digitally signed code and also introduce machine learning models to identify behavioural patterns of applications that act suspiciously. And in this escalated digital arms race, developers of malware are now increasingly turning to artificial intelligence to make their code further undetectable by being designed along more stringent patterns, which of course has triggered security analysts to further enhance their machine learning algorithms' capacity to unveil malicious code. However, so far these acts and counteracts have still not yet fully deployed the capabilities of artificial intelligence tools and big data resources to their full capacity, as far as what is publicly known, but it is a path expected to be fully ensued. Artificial intelligence-enabled malware is designed to be better equipped to familiarise itself with the targeted environment before it sets on an attack, and one must expect harder-to-detect malware, more precisely targeted threats, more convincing phishing, more destructive networkwide infections, more effective methods of propagation, more convincing fake news and clickbaits, and more malware able to operate cross-platform. Some methods that these applications could deploy is to prevent detection by cybersecurity vendors, through deleting itself when it suspects it is being ascertained and analysed, changing shape and form along the way, and deploying malicious activities only on specified systems or individuals. In addition, malware designers could infiltrate and expose security solutions that rely on machine learning to leave certain malicious files alone or generate a large number of false positives, making them appear increasingly unreliable.

Going forward, rather than depend exclusively on security analysts to respond to incidents manually, corporations will, much as the attackers, increasingly rely on artificial intelligence to prepare and imminently respond to digital attacks. This while the human expertise will still manage the strategic oversight and decision-making and perform the remedial work that seeks to improve the overall resilience for the longer term. And also defending algorithms will be configured to re-code themselves, something referred to as adversarial machine learning. Hence, if an adversary tries to attack and infect a server which is located in the internal network, the goal of the adversarial machine learning algorithm is essentially to figure out what is happening and based on the insights dynamically correct and strengthen the network. But to be able to do so, these defensive algorithms can only learn by being exposed to examples and observations of intrusions. Such insights will mostly be obtained through simulated war games of sorts, rather than actual exposures, where hired hackers will try to identify weaknesses in security systems, antivirus software, and other defence measures, by seeking to sneak in undetected and wreak havoc and disable the network. In short, they try to emulate what an enemy might attempt to circumvent against a defence installation and inside a computer system. Typically, they will study software code in detail, looking for flaws that can give them a backdoor into a network, or bypass access controls and obtain unauthorised privileges to manipulate a computer or server. As it is a highly complex and cumbersome process to find security vulnerabilities, and then recognising those bugs that pose a security risk, researchers are developing an automated analysis process for software using a technique known as *symbolic execution* to facilitate this exercise. There is also an interest in combining this symbolic execution with machine learning to create rapid threat analysis, which would allow security analysts to fight off an attack to not just identify the malicious code but to understand its ultimate mission or targets. The goal is to develop techniques that allow highly dynamic portable tools able to respond immediately and autonomously to attacks as they occur.

THE FUTURE: IS INTERNATIONAL LEGISLATION ON THE CARDS?

With digital attacks on the rise and much attribution coming from states that rarely adhere to any international conventions (read: China, North Korea, and Russia), digital warfare for whatever motives where the culprits been able to shun responsibilities have started to become a serious problem to the point that there is an increasing number of voices demanding an internationally binding legislation to be put in place. Hacking into systems to illicitly gather information is no longer merely regarded as espionage as usual but rather as a recklessness that is undermining the whole international system of commerce and beyond. And intellectual property is routinely stolen typically without repercussion to the extent that it is now threatening the very foundation of the knowledge economy. This is often depicted as a distinctly delineated dichotomy between the democratic states of the world vis-à-vis the authoritarian ones with aspirations beyond its borders; however, as the many categories of combatants highlight, there are other vested interests that thrive on operating in what, in part at least, can be described as a lawless environment. Obviously as virtually all countries and industries have been negatively affected by digital warfare and crimes to some extent, only the most gullible corporations are still regarding this threat lightly. But beyond setting up a digital defence and making sure it is maintained and accordingly upgraded, without any legally binding international legislation and a supranational deterrence, countries and corporations alike, even including the US, will not be able to efficiently combat this threat as it is coming from so many disparate forces and in so many forms, which makes it hard to individually combat or regulate. Hence, there is an increasing demand for an international body with judicial power that transcends industries and geographies. But so far, the culprits have been able to constantly identify new security gaps and keep exploiting them for malicious purposes. Notably, this is mainly the hallmarks of the sophisticated state-sponsored attacks, where there appears to be no lack of resources, which increasingly have been augmented by a new generation of artificial intelligence tools. The rising trend of these attacks have not only made sure that they are now a permanent part of the digital landscape but are in fact increasing to the point that they threaten the integrity of the system itself. There are as of yet only a handful of governments capable of launching these wide-scale attacks but have increasingly been doing so and with an improved sophistication. The Microsoft Digital Defense Report, of September 2020, highlighted 14 nation-state groups involved in digital attacks, out of which 11 originate from the previously mentioned three countries. However, with technologies and knowledge becoming widespread, these digital weapons are likely to be proliferated and spread, making monitoring and prevention ever more difficult. Worrisome is also the trend of privatisation of digital warfare, where governments have seen joining forces with outright criminal groups and grey zone private companies focusing on expanding their digital arsenal. It has reached the point where they have become worthy of their own acronym, PSOA (private sector offensive actors). Unlike developing weapons of mass destruction, the engineering of these weapons carries little stigma and certainly no legal consequences so far. And money has been pouring into this sector, where the main bottle neck has been to find enough talented programmers et al. to upgrade malware. To buy digital warriors, even whole armies, has probably never been easier. This has come with severe headaches for individual states, even those as powerful as the US or supranationals like the EU. Thus, calls for an effective global strategy against digital attacks, including legislation, are duly needed. It has to be designed in multiple parts but will also require that governments, governmental agencies, and the technology sector join forces and act in concert when needed. This is a type of warfare requiring a unique level of collaboration between the public and private sectors, as most infrastructure and networks are privately owned. The psychology of warfare which Clausewitz insightfully noted has taught us that deterrence must constitute a key part of such a strategy. A call has been made by representatives from the major democracies of the world and the technology sector to join forces on a number of suggested steps:

- The sharing and analysis of threat intelligence. Given the nature of digital warfare, intelligence must be shared beyond a "need to know" basis towards a pre-empting "need to share" doctrine across substantiated organisations; this must be broadened and established on an international platform in a comprehensive and coordinated manner. Information sharing and collaboration is direly needed for swift and effective action which so far have been difficult to execute.

- The need to strengthen international rules to put reckless countries' behaviour out of bounds and ensure that laws can stifle the increasing trend of digital attacks. International laws and norms should include the continued development of rules to expressly forbid the type of broad and reckless digital warfare activities that have been increasingly noted. Steps have already been taken with a 2015 report by a United Nations Group of Governmental Experts that received broad UN endorsement in 2019, as well as multi-stakeholder support by the Global Commission on the Stability of Cyberspace (GCSC). There are promising initiatives such as the Oxford Process, which has done important work to highlight the protections existing international cyber related laws allow for, and international rules should include stronger protections of democratic and electoral processes, as reflected in the principles of the Paris Call for Trust and Security in Cyberspace. In addition, governments should take new and concerted steps to reel in what is in effect private sector digital armed forces or armouries, which has created a new category of mercenary like combatants to support attacks by state organisations.

- Stronger measures to hold countries accountable for digital attacks. Governments and private companies have started to take concrete action in last few years to hold countries publicly accountable for digital attacks and are now contemplating a framework for legal measures.

- Establish a deterrence capability. Deterrence in effect means dissuading an enemy from an action merely through the threat of force and it can be aimed either at preventing an attack in the first place or preventing an escalation of a hostile situation. Hence, a body administering and overseeing an international legislation needs to be equipped with a credible digital arsenal to enforce, and more importantly through the threat of enforcement, deter potential attackers as they are informed publicly about this armoury and the intent to use it if required. The retaliation threat would be one of the most important non-violent means to make an attacker think twice before deciding to engage in conflict. However, the adverse effect of such a strategy will unfortunately be one of the key rationale that is likely to accelerate the digital arms race.[10,11,12,13,14]

FACT SHEET: WHAT CURRENTLY IS HAPPENING OUT THERE

Unsophisticated attacks work. Most digital attacks are still fairly technically simple. Various types of phishing and social engineering are attack vectors that have proven to work also against organisations priding themselves on focusing on high levels of security.

Fast attacks work. Attacks designed to exploit known security vulnerabilities have proven to be surprisingly successful, this as many organisations are slow to update their security arrangements, nor do they isolate systems with recently ascertained vulnerabilities. This time lag in upgrading systems provides a window of opportunity for digital attackers quick to adjust their digital arsenal to use newly publicised weaknesses as entry points.

Advanced attacks work. There is a tier of very advanced digital weapons being launched, as described in this book which still very few organisation have prepared adequate defences against.

Opportunistic attacks work. Attackers of all types have been able to quickly and in an opportunistic way, adjust their weapons in accordance with societal trends, such as the Covid-19 pandemic, including tools for social manipulation, software, and bogus websites.

Basic security measures work. Many digital attacks, also sophisticated ones, have been mitigated or prevented through relatively simple security arrangements. Organisations consistently maintaining and upgrading their security routines might be affected, but usually suffer less severe consequences.

Nation-states tend to focus on espionage rather than sabotage. The main focus of nation-states is intrusion into systems or the distribution of spyware, with a view to obtain classified information of a military, economic, or technical nature. They are also gathering information about individuals, including activity and positioning data from mobile equipment. They are targeting a wide range of targets, such as governments, military units, political parties, and corporations in most industries. There are indications that these broad-brushed methods mean that their intelligence gathering tools lack precision, and they are applying a shotgun approach to identify opportunities.

Attackers are utilising suppliers and third-party services. Websites, equipment, and tools as part of the network infrastructure and upgrading mechanisms are sought after intrusion points for an attacker seeking vectors for future espionage and sabotage.

The organisations and methods for digital warfare are being refined. Specialisation and increased refinements of capabilities are advancing the digital warfare setup. Certain hacker groups might focus on particular industries targeting their idiosyncratic peculiarities, and they might act in concert by being in charge of different tasks of the attack.

Digital warfare is being commercialised. Commercial ventures are cropping up focused on developing different types of digital weapons: spyware, trojans, and other malware, accompanied by programmers working on contracts to embed these weapons into arsenals preparing for digital attacks. These corporations often actively recruit cyber soldiers that have previously served in military units or security forces.

Digital attacks have become an integrated part of hybrid warfare. Recently, some countries have used digital attacks as a response to physical attacks. In other cases, they have been the preferred response to digital attacks. Mostly, they have not tried to deny responsibility, if not always officially admitted.

Cooperation among the different types of combatants. It appears that some countries are cooperating with private hacker groups, at times acting as affiliates, and at other times operating independently. In essence, being part criminals and part state-sponsored digital warriors.

Law enforcements are upping their games. Law enforcements such as FBI and Europol have started to more aggressively pursue digital attackers, and a number of individuals have been charged for cybercrimes; it is considered that they have conducted acting for state organisations.

Source: Lindahl, David. *Omvärldsbevakning: Statsattribuerade cyberoperationer* 2020 (FOI Memo 7422, 2020-12-18).

NOTES

1 Kahneman, Daniel. A Perspective on Judgment and Choice: Mapping Bounded Rationality (*American Psychologist*, Vol. 58 (2003)). pp. 697–720.

2 Chotikul, Diane. Soviet Theory of Reflexive Control in Historical and Psychocultural Perspective: A Preliminary Study (Naval Postgraduate School, Monterey, California, 1986).

3 Vosoughi, Soroush, Roy, Deb, & Aral, Sinan. The Spread of True and False News Online (*Science*, Vol. 359, Issue 6380 (09 Mar 2018)). pp. 1146–1151.

4 Chandler, Daniel & Munday, Rod. *A Dictionary of Media and Communication, The Thomas Theorem* (Oxford: Oxford University Press, 2011).

5 Metz, Cade. *Finally, a Machine That Can Finish Your Sentence* (New York Times, 7 June 2019). https://www.nytimes.com/2018/11/18/technology/artificial-intelligence-language.html (accessed 1 January 2021).

6 Paul, Christopher, & Posard, Marek N. *Artificial Intelligence and the Manufacturing of Reality* (The Rand Blog, 20 January 2020). https://www.rand.org/blog/2020/01/artificial-intelligence-and-the-manufacturing-of-reality.html#1 (accessed 1 January 2021).

7 Thomas, Timothy. Russia's Reflexive Control Theory and the Military (*Journal of Slavic Military Studies*, Vol. 17, Issue 2 (2004)). pp. 237–256.

8 Barber, Gregory. *Deepfakes Are Getting Better, But They're Still Easy to Spot* (Wired, 26 May 2019). https://www.wired.com/story/deepfakes-getting-better-theyre-easy-spot/ (accessed 1 January 2021).

9 Leonenko, S. Refleksivnoe upravlenie protivnikom [Reflexive control of the enemy] (*Armeiskii sbornik* (*Army Collection*), No. 8 (1995)). p. 28.

10 Smith, Brad. *A Moment of Reckoning: The Need for a Strong and Global Cybersecurity Response* (Microsoft on the Issues. The Official Microsoft Blog, 17 December 2020). https://blogs.microsoft.com/on-the-issues/2020/12/17/cyberattacks-cybersecurity-solarwinds-fireeye/ (accessed 1 January 2021).

11 United Nations General Assembly. *74/28. Advancing Responsible State behaviour in Cyberspace in the Context of International Security* (Seventy-fourth session Agenda item 93 Developments in the field of information and telecommunications in the context of international security, Resolution adopted by the General Assembly on 12 December 2019). https://undocs.org/A/RES/74/28 (accessed 1 January 2021).

12 Global Commission on the Stability of Cyberspace. *Advancing Cyberstability Final Report* (November 2019). https://cyberstability.org/report/ (accessed 1 January 2021).

13 Oxford Institute for Ethics, Law and Armed Conflict. *The Oxford Statement on the International Law Protections against Cyber Operations Targeting the Health Care Sector* (Blavatnik School of Government, University of Oxford). https://www.elac.ox.ac.uk/the-oxford-statement-on-the-international-law-protections-against-cyber-operations-targeting-the-hea (accessed 1 January 2021).

14 Paris Call. *Paris Call. For Trust and Security in Cyberspace.* (Paris Call, 11 December 2018). https://pariscall.international/en/ (accessed 1 January 2021).

REFERENCES

Barber, Gregory. *Deepfakes Are Getting Better, But They're Still Easy to Spot* (Wired, 26 May 2019). https://www.wired.com/story/deepfakes-getting-better-theyre-easy-spot/ (accessed 1 January 2021).

Bassford, Christopher. *Policy, Politics, War, and Military Strategy* (The Clausewitz Homepage, 1997–2015). http://www.clausewitz.com/readings/Bassford/StrategyDraft/index.htm (accessed 1 January 2021).

Beyerchen, Alan D. Clausewitz, Nonlinearity and the Unpredictability of War (*International Security*, Vol. 17, Issue 3 (Winter, 1992–1993)).

Borys, Christian. *Ukraine Braces for Further Cyber-Attacks* (BBC News, 25 July 2017). https://www.bbc.com/news/technology-40706093 (accessed 1 January 2021).

Chandler, Daniel & Munday, Rod. *A Dictionary of Media and Communication, The Thomas Theorem* (Oxford: Oxford University Press, 2011).

Cheng, Dean. *Cyber Dragon: Inside China's Information Warfare and Cyber Operations* (Westport, CT: Praeger Security International, 2017).

Chotikul, Diane. *Soviet Theory of Reflexive Control in Historical and Psychocultural Perspective: A Preliminary Study* (Monterey, CA: Naval Postgraduate School, 1986).

Citino, Robert M. *The German Way of War: From the Thirty Years' War to the Third Reich* (Lawrence: University of Kansas Press. 2005).

Corum, James S. *The Roots of Blitzkrieg: Hans von Seeckt and German Military Reform* (Modern War Studies. Lawrence: University Press of Kansas, 1992).

Cybersecurity & Infrastructure Security Agency. *Alert (AA20–280A) Emotet Malware* (National Cyber Awareness System, 6 October 2020). https://us-cert.cisa.gov/ncas/alerts/aa20-280a (accessed 1 January 2021).

Department of Homeland Security/Cybersecurity & Infrastructure Security Agency. *Understanding Denial-of-Service Attacks* (Security Tip ST04-015, 04 November 2009). https://us-cert.cisa.gov/ncas/tips/ST04-015 (accessed 1 January 2021).

Doob, Leonard W. The Strategies of Psychological Warfare (*Public Opinion Quarterly*, Vol. 13, Issue 4, (1949)). pp. 635–644.

Ellul, Jacques. *Propaganda: The Formation of Men's Attitudes* ([Propagandes] Translated by Konrad Kellen & Jean Lerner from original 1962 French edition. New York: Vintage Books, 1973).

Emerging Technology from the arXivarchive page. *The First DDoS Attack Was 20 Years Ago. This Is What We've Learned Since* (MIT Technology Review, 18 April 2019). https://www.technologyreview.com/2019/04/18/103186/the-first-ddos-attack-was-20-years-ago-this-is-what-weve-learned-since/ (accessed 1 January 2021).

Frieser, Karl-Heinz. *The Blitzkrieg Legend: The 1940 Campaign in the West* ([Blitzkrieg-legende: der westfeldzug 1940] trans. J. T. Greenwood. Annapolis, MD: Naval Institute Press, 2005).

Fruhlinger, Josh. *What is WannaCry Ransomware, How Does It Infect, and Who Was Responsible?* (CSO, 30 August 2018). https://www.csoonline.com/article/3227906/what-is-wannacry-ransomware-how-does-it-infect-and-who-was-responsible.html (accessed 1 January 2021).

Global Commission on the Stability of Cyberspace. *Advancing Cyberstability Final Report* (November 2019). https://cyberstability.org/report/ (accessed 1 January 2021).

Google Official Blog. *A New Approach to China* (12 January 2010). https://googleblog.blogspot.com/2010/01/new-approach-to-china.html (accessed 1 January 2021).

Greenberg, Andy. *Petya Ransomware Epidemic May Be Spillover From Cyberwar* (Wired Magazine, 28 June 2017). https://www.wired.com/story/petya-ransomware-ukraine/ (accessed 1 January 2021).

Greenberg, Andy. *The Untold Story of NotPetya, the Most Devastating Cyberattack in History* (Wired Magazine, 22 August 2018). https://www.wired.com/story/notpetya-cyberattack-ukraine-russia-code-crashed-the-world/ (accessed 1 January 2021).

Griffin, Andrew. *Cyber Attack: Chernobyl's Radiation Monitoring System Hit by Worldwide Hack* (The Independent, 27 June 2017). https://www.independent.co.uk/news/world/europe/chernobyl-ukraine-petya-cyber-attack-hack-nuclear-power-plant-danger-latest-a7810941.html (accessed 1 January 2021).

Haizler, Omry. The United States' Cyber Warfare History: Implications on Modern Cyber Operational Structures and Policymaking (*The Institute for National Security Studies. Cyber, Intelligence, and Security*, Vol. 1, Issue 1, January 2017). https://www.inss.org.il/he/wp-content/uploads/sites/2/system-files/The%20United%20States%E2%80%99%20Cyber%20Warfare%20History%20Implications%20on.pdf (accessed 1 January 2021).

Headquarters; Department of the Army. *Appendix I: PSYOP Techniques* (Psychological Operations Field Manual No. 33-1, 31 August 1979).

Hosseini-Asl, Ehsan, Zhou, Yingbo, Xiong, Caiming, & Socher, Richard. *A Multi-Discriminator CycleGAN for Unsupervised Non-Parallel Speech Domain Adaptation* (Salesforce Research, 9 July 2018). https://arxiv.org/pdf/1804.00522.pdf (accessed 1 January 2021).

Jowett, Garth S., & O'Donnell, Victoria. *Propaganda & Persuasion* (Thousand Oaks, CA: SAGE Publications, Inc., 5th edition, 2011).

Kahneman, Daniel. A Perspective on Judgment and Choice: Mapping Bounded Rationality (*American Psychologist*, Vol. 58 (2003)). pp. 697–720.

Karlins, Marvin, & Abelson, Herbet I. *Persuasion: How Opinions and Attitudes Are Changed* (New York: Springer, 2nd edition, 1970).

Kilcullen, David. *The Accidental Guerrilla: Fighting Small Wars in the Midst of a Big One* (Oxford: Oxford University Press, Reprint Edition, 2011).

Lando, Gabriel. *Machine Vs. Machine. A Look at AI-powered Ransomware* (FileCloud Blog, 27 August 2018). https://www.getfilecloud.com/blog/2018/08/machine-vs-machine-a-look-at-ai-powered-ransomware/#.X-McsthK-g2w (accessed 1 January 2021).

Leonenko, S. Refleksivnoe upravlenie protivnikom [Reflexive control of the enemy] (*Armeiskii sbornik* (*Army Collection*), Issue 8, 1995). p. 28.

Lerner, Daniel. *Psychological Warfare against Nazi Germany: The Sykewar Campaign, D-Day to VE-Day* (Boston, MA: MIT Press, 1971).

Lind, William S. *Understanding Fourth Generation War* (15 January 2004). www.antiwar.com (accessed 1 January 2021).

Lind, William S., Nightengale, Keith, Schmitt, John F., Sutton, Joseph W., Wilson, Gary I. The Changing Face of War: Into the Fourth Generation (*Marine Corps Gazette*, October 1989). pp. 22–26.

Messmer, Ellen. *Serb Supporters Sock It to NATO, U.S. Web Sites* (CNN, 6 April 1999). http://edition.cnn.com/TECH/computing/9904/06/serbnato.idg/index.html (accessed 1 January 2021).

Metz, Cade. *Finally, a Machine That Can Finish Your Sentence* (New York Times, 7 June 2019).

Nakashima, Ellen. *Russian Military Was Behind 'NotPetya' Cyberattack in Ukraine, CIA Concludes* (Washington Post, 13 January 2018). https://www.washingtonpost.com/world/national-security/russian-military-was-behind-notpetya-cyberattack-in-ukraine-cia-concludes/2018/01/12/048d8506-f7ca-11e7-b34a-b85626af34ef_story.html (accessed 1 January 2021).

Nakashima, Ellen, & Warrick, Joby. *Stuxnet Was Work of U.S. and Israeli Experts, Officials Say* (Washington Post, 2 June 2012). https://www.washingtonpost.com/world/national-security/stuxnet-was-work-of-us-and-israeli-experts-officials-say/2012/06/01/gJQAInEy6U_story.html (accessed 1 January 2021).

Naveh, Shimon. *In Pursuit of Military Excellence: The Evolution of Operational Theory* (London: Frank Cass, 1997).

Oxford Institute for Ethics, Law and Armed Conflict. *The Oxford Statement on the International Law Protections Against Cyber Operations Targeting the Health Care Sector* (Blavatnik School of Government, University of Oxford). https://www.elac.ox.ac.uk/the-oxford-statement-on-the-international-law-protections-against-cyber-operations-targeting-the-hea (accessed 1 January 2021).

Paris Call. *Paris Call. For Trust and Security in Cyberspace* (Paris Call, 11 December 2018). https://pariscall.international/en/ (accessed 1 January 2021).

Paul, Christopher, & Posard, Marek N. *Artificial Intelligence and the Manufacturing of Reality* (The Rand Blog, 20 January 2020). https://www.rand.org/blog/2020/01/artificial-intelligence-and-the-manufacturing-of-reality.html#1 (accessed 1 January 2021).

Pratkanis, Anthony, & Aronson, Elliot. *Age of Propaganda:-The Everyday Use and Abuse of Persuasion* (New York: Holt Paperbacks, 2001).

Qualter, Terence H. *Propaganda and Psychological Warfare* (Studies in Political Science. New York: Random House, 1962).

Rhode, B. (ed.). *Artificial Intelligence and Offensive Cyber Weapon* (Strategic Comments, Vol. 25, Issue 10 (2019)).

Satter, Raphael. *Experts: Spy Used AI-Generated Face to Connect with Targets* (New York: Associated Press, 13 June 2019). https://apnews.com/article/bc2f19097a4c4fffaa00de6770b8a60d (accessed 1 January 2021).

Sheehan, Matt. *How Google Took on China—And Lost* (MIT Technology Review, 19 December 2018). https://www.technologyreview.com/2018/12/19/138307/how-google-took-on-china-and-lost/#:~:-text=Google's%20first%20foray%20into%20Chinese,over%20censorship%20of%20search%20results (accessed 1 January 2021).

Smith, Brad. *A Moment of Reckoning: The Need for a Strong and Global Cybersecurity Response* (Microsoft on the Issues. The Official Microsoft Blog, 17 December 2020). https://blogs.microsoft.com/on-the-issues/2020/12/17/cyberattacks-cybersecurity-solarwinds-fireeye/ (accessed 1 January 2021).

Stoecklin, Marc Ph. *DeepLocker: How AI Can Power a Stealthy New Breed of Malware* (Security Intelligence, 8 August 2018). https://securityintelligence.com/deeplocker-how-ai-can-power-a-stealthy-new-breed-of-malware/ (accessed 1 January 2021).

Svensson, Erik, Magnusson, Jonas, & Zuave, Erik. *Kryptomaskar och deras konsekvenser Åtgärder för cybersäkerhet utifrån fallen WannaCry och NotPetya* (FOI-R-4774-SE, ISSN 1650-1942, FOI, June 2019).

Szunyogh, Béla. *Psychological Warfare; An Introduction to Ideological Propaganda and the Techniques of Psychological Warfare* (New York: William-Frederick Press, 1955).

The European Union Agency for Cybersecurity (ENISA). *ENISA Overview of Cybersecurity and Related Terminology* (September 2017). https://www.enisa.europa.eu/publications/enisa-position-papers-and-opinions/enisa-overview-of-cybersecurity-and-related-terminology (accessed 1 January 2021).

Thomas, Timothy. *Russia's Reflexive Control Theory and the Military* (Journal of Slavic Military Studies, Vol. 17, Issue 2 (2004)). pp. 237–256.

Thornton, Rod. *Asymmetric Warfare* (Malden, MA: Polity Press, 2007).

Tikk, Eneken, Kaska, Kadri, & Vihul, Liis. *International Cyber Incidents: Legal Considerations* (2010). https://ccdcoe.org/library/publications/international-cyber-incidents-legal-considerations/ (accessed 1 January 2021).

Trinquier, Roger. *Modern Warfare: A French View of Counterinsurgency* (Leavenworth, KS: Army University Press, 1961). https://www.armyupress.army.mil/Portals/7/combat-studies-institute/csi-books/Modern-Warfare.pdf (accessed 1 January 2021).

United Nations General Assembly. 74/28. *Advancing Responsible State behaviour in Cyberspace in the Context of International Security* (Seventy-fourth session Agenda item 93 Developments in the field of information and telecommunications in the context of international security, Resolution adopted by the General Assembly on 12 December 2019). https://undocs.org/A/RES/74/28 (accessed 1 January 2021).

US Department of Justice, U.S. Attorney's Office, Eastern District of New York. *Two International Cybercriminal Rings Dismantled and Eight Defendants Indicted for Causing Tens of Millions of Dollars in Losses in Digital Advertising Fraud* (27 November 2018). https://www.justice.gov/usao-edny/pr/two-international-cybercriminal-rings-dismantled-and-eight-defendants-indicted-causing (accessed 1 January 2021).

Valery, Gerasimov. *The Value of Science in Prediction* (Military-Industrial Kurier, 27 February 2013). https://vpk-news.ru/sites/default/files/pdf/VPK_08_476.pdf; translation downloaded from IES https://www.ies.be/files/Gerasimov%20HW%20ENG.pdf (accessed 1 January 2021).

Vest, Jason. *Fourth-generation Warfare* (The Atlantic, 01 December 2001).

von Clausewitz, Carl. *On War* ([*Vom Kriege*] Editor and translator Howard, Michael; Paret, Peter, Princeton, NJ: Princeton University Press (1989) [1832]).

Vosoughi, Soroush, Roy, Deb & Aral, Sinan. The Spread of True and False News Online (*Science*, Vol. 359, Issue 6380 (09 March 2018)). pp. 1146–1151.

Wadell, Kaveh. *The Computer Virus That Haunted Early AIDS Researchers* (The Atlantic, 10 May 2016). https://www.theatlantic.com/technology/archive/2016/05/the-computer-virus-that-haunted-early-aids-researchers/481965/ (accessed 1 January 2021).

INDEX

Note: *Italic* page numbers refer to figures and page number followed by "n" refer to end notes.

Printed in the United States
by Baker & Taylor Publisher Services

Printed in the United States
by Baker & Taylor Publisher Services